52 PRAYERS FOR MY FUTURE WIFE

TYNDALE
MOMENTUM™

A Tyndale nonfiction imprint

52 PRAYERS FOR MY FUTURE WIFE

A DEVOTIONAL

CALEB ROUSE

Visit Tyndale online at tyndale.com.

52 Prayers for My Future Wife: A Devotional

Published in association with The Bindery Agency, www.TheBinderyAgency.com.

Cover design by Ellery Sterling

Interior design by Laura Cruise

Edited by Sarah Kelley

For information about special discounts for bulk purchases, please contact Tyndale House Publishers at csresponse@tyndale.com, or call 1-855-277-9400.

ISBN 979-8-4005-2334-2

Printed in China

32 31 30 29 28 27 26

7 6 5 4 3 2 1

To my amazing wife, Stefanie:

You bring so much joy to my life and are the woman of my dreams. I am so thankful God made me wait for you. You were worth every second that I waited. I love you.

To Chad, Matthew, Tobius, Brant, Karl, Victor, Sunjay, Jason, Steven, James, and all our beloved community:

It's been the joy and honor of my life to walk beside you as you honor God in the way you live out singleness, dating, and marriage. Thanks for letting me walk beside you.

Introduction

Dear brother,

If you're holding this book, I imagine you have a dream in your heart. A dream for love. A dream for partnership. A dream to build a marriage rooted in faith and Christ's love.

Maybe you're single, praying for the woman you haven't met yet. Maybe you're dating and wondering if this relationship might be "the one." Maybe you're engaged and preparing for one of the biggest commitments of your life with both joy and nervous anticipation. Or maybe you've walked through heartbreak, disappointment, or even divorce, and you're wondering if God can still redeem your story.

Wherever you are on your journey, this book is for you.

As men, many of us grow up with hopes of finding a wife, building a family, and stepping into a bigger purpose. Maybe you've pictured your wedding day, imagined the joy of seeing your bride walk down the aisle, or dreamed about the life you'll build together. But you wonder when that day will come or if God cares about your dreams.

That's the heart behind this devotional: to help you trust God with your future wife while also letting Him shape you into the man He's called you to be.

God Sees You

Here's the truth you need to hold on to: God sees you. He sees your tears and your longings. He knows the desires of your heart. And He hasn't forgotten you. Even when it feels quiet, He's working. He's writing a story far better than the one you might be trying to write for yourself.

I know what it feels like to wonder if love has passed you by. To wrestle with questions like *Will I ever meet her? Did I miss my chance? Did I mess up too badly?* I've asked those questions myself. But the waiting and setbacks weren't wasted. God was shaping me, pruning me, and preparing me to one day be a husband. And the same is true for you.

Why Pray for Your Future Wife?

If you are single, maybe you're wondering why you should pray for someone you haven't met yet. The answer is this: Prayer doesn't just change circumstances; it changes us. When you pray for your future wife, you're not only asking God to prepare her; you're asking Him to prepare you. You're surrendering your desires to His will, allowing Him to heal your heart, sharpen your character, and align your life with His purpose.

Prayer is not weak. It's not passive. It's powerful. Every prayer is a seed planted into your future. Even when you can't see the results, God is tending to the seeds and cultivating something extraordinary beneath the surface. And the greatest gift of prayer is that it pulls you closer to Jesus. Marriage is a blessing, but it can't complete you. Only Christ can do that. The more secure you are in Him, the more ready you'll be to love your wife with strength, patience, and grace.

Finally, prayer is powerful. God sees your future wife. He knows the challenges she faces, the pain she carries, and the prayers she's lifting up. Your intercession matters. Your prayers may be protecting her, strengthening her, and preparing her heart.

How to Use This Devotional

This book is designed to guide you, whether you're in a season of waiting or already preparing for marriage. Each devotional includes the following:

- **Scripture**
  Each week begins with a verse that ties to the theme. God's Word is alive; it's what strengthens us when our doubts begin whispering or when the waiting season feels tiresome. Take time to read it slowly, pray over it, and commit it to memory. Let it anchor you.
- **A Devotion**
  You'll find a reflection—sometimes from my own journey or from lessons God has shown me—that connects to the topic. These are here to remind you that you're not alone and to point you back to God's faithfulness.

- **Prayer**

  Each devotional includes a prayer for your future wife and yourself. You can pray them as written or make them your own. Don't worry about sounding perfect; God wants your heart, not polished words.

- **Love in Action**

  Prayer should move us to action. That's why each week ends with a simple step to live out what you're praying. Sometimes it's personal, like journaling or practicing gratitude. Other times, it's reaching outward, like sharing encouraging words with someone, serving in a ministry, or choosing forgiveness. These small acts are seeds that will one day bless your marriage.

- **Encouragement**

  Finally, there's a short word of encouragement to carry into your week. Write it down, keep it close, and let it remind you of what God is doing.

You can use this book for fifty-two weeks, turning it into a yearlong journey, or daily if you would like a shorter journey. You may also go through it with a trusted friend for accountability. However you use it, the goal is not speed but depth.

The Heart Behind This Book

This devotional isn't about trying to earn a wife or rush God's timeline. It's about walking with Him daily, trusting His plan, and allowing Him to shape you while you wait. My prayer is that as you work through the devotions, you'll grow closer to

Him. When you're secure in Christ, you'll be able to love your wife not from emptiness, but from strength and wholeness.

A Blessing for You

As you begin this journey, here's a blessing for you:

> May this devotional become a space where you bring your hopes, heartbreaks, and prayers before God. May each week remind you that you are seen, loved, and chosen. May you grow in strength, patience, and faith—qualities that will bless not only your future marriage, but also every relationship in your life. And may you trust that God's timing is perfect. He knows how to bring the right woman into your life at the right time, and He knows how to prepare you to be the kind of husband who reflects His love.

A Prayer for You

> **Heavenly Father,** *I lift up my brother who is reading this book. You know his heart. You know his longings, his disappointments, and his dreams. Thank You that he is not forgotten but fully seen and deeply loved by You.*
>
> *Lord, I ask that as he walks through these pages, You would meet him in a powerful way. Heal the places of his heart that are hurting. Strengthen his faith where doubt has crept in. Fill him with hope, courage, and patience as he waits for Your perfect timing.*

Prepare him to love like You love—sacrificially, faithfully, and with grace. Shape him into the man You've created him to be, so that one day he may be a blessing to his future wife and a reflection of Christ in their marriage.

But most of all, let him fall more in love with You in this season. Let his security and joy be found in You alone. May his waiting not be wasted, but instead be a time of growth and intimacy with You.

Bless his future marriage, his future wife, and the story You are writing. Bless him today as You work in his life, making him a deeper reflection of You. In Jesus' name, amen.

Your waiting is not wasted. Your prayers are not wasted. And your story is not over. With many blessings,

Caleb Rouse
Christian relationship mentor

WEEK

1

GOD'S PLAYBOOK BEATS MINE EVERY TIME

We can make our plans,
but the LORD determines our steps.
PROVERBS 16:9

Growing up, my dreams were simple: get married, have a family, and play professional basketball. I chased those dreams with everything I had. Throughout high school I poured myself into sports, and I was in a long-term relationship that carried into college. By God's grace, I earned a scholarship to play basketball at the collegiate level and pushed even harder toward my goal of playing professionally overseas.

But then, during my senior year, everything began falling apart. My girlfriend of five years, whom I thought I would marry, ended our relationship. Amid this heartbreak, I lost my first grandparent, my grandfather, and his passing crushed me. Then, just before my senior season, I suffered a back injury that shattered my hopes of ever playing basketball professionally. I was devastated. I lost sight of my purpose and even questioned God's love for me. In my mind, if He really cared, He wouldn't have taken everything away.

But as I worked through the pain of each loss and surrendered my future to Him, my perspective changed. I began to trust that God's playbook was better than mine. His purpose for my life was greater than anything I could have planned.

And He had someone in store for me, my wife, Stefanie, who would far exceed my greatest dreams. God has a way of turning pain into purpose. In His timing, He takes the dreams we cling to and expands them into His greater plan. Don't lose hope in the waiting. God will lead you step-by-step. Trust Him and pursue Him in the process.

Dear heavenly Father, *I lift up my future wife's dreams, desires, and plans to You. As she waits on You, give her peace and wisdom in her decisions, and guide her deeper into Your purpose. When disappointment comes, fill her with hope and turn her heart toward Your Word. When adversity rises, help her to stand on Your truth and endure the storms the enemy may bring.*

Lord, prepare me in the same way. Heal my heart so I can be gentle, patient, and understanding with hers. Make me a safe place for her in the future. Grant me wisdom in my choices so I may draw closer to You and the purpose You've set for my life. Teach us both to find our worth in You alone, and in Your perfect timing, guide our hearts toward each other. In Jesus' name, amen.

Love in Action . . .

Write down one dream or area of your life where you've been trying to force your own way. Pray over it and hand it back to God. Trust His playbook over your own.

God's playbook never loses.

WEEK

2 TRAIN WHILE YOU WAIT

No discipline is enjoyable while it is happening—it's painful! But afterward there will be a peaceful harvest of right living for those who are trained in this way.

HEBREWS 12:11

I grew up in a Christian home, attending church and Sunday school on the weekends and Christian schools on the weekdays. From a young age, I knew God was the foundation for my life, and I truly loved Him. But as I got older, one thing was missing: the habit of reading my Bible. Sure, I would open it at youth group and on retreats, or when I felt especially "spiritual," but my time spent in God's Word wasn't consistent.

After college, I struggled with discouragement, bouts of depression, and addictions to pornography and video games. My mindset was firm: *I know enough about God. I'm good.* But the truth was, I wasn't good. My faith was weak, my beliefs were shaky, and I was drowning in sin and desperation. If there is one habit I wish I had started sooner, it would be reading my Bible daily. When I finally made that decision, everything changed.

I started small, one verse from the book of Psalms each day. Just one. Over time, that simple discipline grew into a rhythm of digesting entire chapters. As I built this daily habit, God began to transform me. The addictions and struggles that once held me started to loosen their grip, and my mind, body, and spirit began to experience freedom. Sure, I still face challenges and temptations today, but my foundation is secure in Christ. I know where to turn first when struggles come—not to myself, but to the truth of God's Word. He is good. Always.

Dear God, *thank You for always reaching out to me, reminding me of who You are, of who I am, and that I am never alone. Please remind my future wife of this truth today. Help her to develop good habits in this season that draw her closer to You. Prompt her to spend time in Your Word, and let Your truth sink deeply into her heart. Father, guide her in building healthy rhythms, not just spiritually, but also physically, financially, and in community. Give her wisdom and the strength to stay consistent. When she feels overwhelmed, surround her with Your peace that surpasses all understanding. Be her provider and sustain her as she grows into the woman You've called her to be. When the enemy throws lies or temptations her way, cover her and protect her under the shadow of Your wings.*

And Lord, do the same work in me. Help me to develop good habits that prepare me to be a faithful, loving husband. Show me the areas where I need to grow, and give me endurance through the growing pains so I can become the man You've called me to be. Thank You for Your unfailing love. You are so good. Amen.

Love in Action . . .

Do twenty minutes of focused training today, whether it's lifting weights, reading a chapter of the Bible, or creating a budget. Build the disciplines now that you desire to carry into marriage later.

The man I'm becoming today shapes the husband I'll be tomorrow.

WEEK

3

PATIENCE IS STRENGTH UNDER CONTROL

If we look forward to something we don't yet have, we must wait patiently and confidently.

ROMANS 8:25

I've always had a love-hate relationship with running. I know it's good for me, but I've never enjoyed it. Give me a ball, a court, or a paddle—anything but *just* running. Growing up, my dad was the cross-country coach at my high school. When I was a freshman and the fall season rolled around, I had a choice to make: wait for him after practice every day or join the team and use the time as conditioning for other sports. I chose the latter.

My dad was a legend in the sport, and his teams were always strong. When I first joined, I quickly found out why. They trained hard, fast, and *a lot*. Running taught me patience, especially on the days when our afternoon runs ranged anywhere from five to twelve miles. My dad never told us how far we'd go or which route we'd take. We had no phones and no way to track our distance; we just had to run together until he said, "Stop." I hated not knowing. Even worse, if we asked, he would often add distance just to stretch us.

But in the process, I learned to be patient, to lean on teammates, and to depend on God for strength. The runs brought challenges, long hills, steep downhills, blisters, and cramps. But they also brought beauty: flowers, mountains, quiet trails, and a sense of achievement. Not every run was long, but each practice prepared us. Through it all, my dad protected us, had our best interests in mind, and was training us for something greater. God works the same way. He knows the route, the distance, and the encounters ahead of us. Just as I had to trust my dad, we are called to trust Him.

As you wait on your future spouse, ask, *What is God teaching me in this season?* His path ends with a prize, given in His perfect way and timing.

—

Heavenly Father, *thank You for the ways You are protecting me and my future wife. Waiting is never easy, especially when I can't see the steps ahead, but today I choose to trust You. Guide my future wife down the path You've set for her. Show her that You are with her, and help her notice the beauty beside her. Give her purpose in this season, and open her eyes to see the plan You have for her. When she grows tired, hold her up. When she gets frustrated, give her hope. And when she feels like giving up, show her the way forward.*

I ask that You provide people to encourage her, point her back to You, and lift her up in difficult times. As she trusts You, make her path straight. Train her in the way she should go, shaping her into a woman of wisdom, strength, and faith. Prepare her to be both a godly wife and a devoted follower of Jesus. And Lord, as she waits, develop in her the mind of Christ. Shape us both to glorify You with our lives. In Jesus' name, amen.

Love in Action . . .

Next time your impatience rises, stop and take a deep breath. Pray Psalm 37:7: “Be still before the LORD and wait patiently for him” (ESV).

Patience leads to God's perfect path for you.

WEEK

4

DELAY ISN'T DEFEAT

The smallest family will become a thousand people,
and the tiniest group will become a mighty nation.
At the right time, I, the Lord, will make it happen.
ISAIAH 60:22

Waiting for the woman God has for you can feel a lot like being stuck at the airport. You know the destination, and you're excited to get there, but waiting at the terminal is the last place you want to be. Delays can stir discouragement and anxiety. For many years, I prayed to meet my wife. Honestly, I bargained with God plenty of times. After each breakup or setback, I felt more anxious and defeated.

Delays can even feel like closed doors. You meet someone, maybe even have a real connection, only to realize they're not "the one." That heartbreak can feel final—I know it well. After my five-year relationship ended, I thought my story was over. I questioned God's plan. What I learned through the process, however, is the more I surrendered my desires and emotions to God, the clearer my vision grew, and the more peace I found in the present. God was preparing me for the next chapter.

The moment I fully released my hopes and desires to Him was the moment my wife, Stefanie, walked into my life. I first saw her at church, and I knew she was the type of woman God had in mind for me. Even then, though, I had to wait. She was dating someone else. That delay tested me again, but this time I had hope. One year later, after her relationship ended, we went on our first date. A year after that, we were married. Friend, God isn't late. He's always on time, waiting for us to give Him our whole hearts. Our delays are not defeat; they're preparation.

Heavenly Father, *waiting can sometimes feel like defeat. When doors close, I often get discouraged. Please forgive me for the times I've failed to trust You fully, and restore my hope today.*

I pray for my future wife. Strengthen her in this season. Whatever delay she is facing, help her surrender it to You. Fill her mind with peace, her heart with courage, and her steps with wisdom. Remind her of the blessings already around her, and open her eyes to see them with gratitude. Prepare her to be a godly wife who can walk with me through hard seasons and point me back to You. Guide her steps in a way that draws us closer together, and grant us both patience and peace in the journey. Waiting is hard, but with Your strength, all things are possible. In Jesus' name, amen.

Love in Action . . .

Write down one prayer that feels unanswered. Beside it, write about a time God came through for you. Let His past wins build your present faith.

Delay doesn't mean defeat;
it means preparation.

WEEK

5

ANOTHER MAN'S WIN DOESN'T STEAL YOURS

Be happy with those who are happy, and weep with those who weep.

ROMANS 12:15

If I'm honest, one of the hardest parts of my singleness journey was watching other people get married. With the rise of social media during those years, I was constantly bombarded with highlight reels of others' proposals and engagements, and they could send me spiraling. When friends from college or high school announced their upcoming weddings, jealousy hit me hard. I'd find myself pleading with God. *Why not me? Where is my love story?* Out of pain, I didn't want to celebrate others in their joy.

If you've ever asked those same questions, you're not alone. More importantly, your story is not over. I've learned that when we refuse to celebrate others' joy, bitterness and resentment grow quickly. But when we choose to lift others up, even in our waiting, it breeds hope. It helps us love others the way we want to be loved. When I chose to celebrate my friends and family at their weddings instead of choosing not to go, I received the blessing of being encouraged by their stories. Those moments became catalysts for God's promises that I held on to in my own waiting. Seeing their joy brought me inspiration to not quit and keep trusting God for more.

Someone else's joy doesn't mean your story has been forgotten or stolen. God's plan for each one of us is unique and beautiful. His timing may not align with ours, but it doesn't erase His goodness. Your story is still unfolding, and in the meantime, look around and see how truly blessed you already are.

Dear God, *thank You for the blessings You've already given me and for the ways You've protected me. Please give me peace and contentment as I wait on You. I pray for my future wife. Cover her with Your grace and love as she carries the desires of her heart. Comfort her in disappointment, and give her the strength to rejoice with others when they celebrate the things she longs for. Fill her heart with gratitude for what she has, even while she waits for what's to come. Prepare both of us to trust You with every new desire we'll face in marriage. Reveal any bitterness that may have taken root, and help us fully surrender it to You. Teach us to celebrate others without comparison, knowing that Your plans for us are good. Thank You for everything You've already done to prepare us for the future. Continue shaping us until the day we finally meet. In the mighty name of Jesus, amen.*

Love in Action . . .

Celebrate a friend's good news—whether it's an engagement, marriage, or new job. Send them a text or pray for them. Their win isn't a loss for you.

Another man's blessing doesn't steal mine.

WEEK

6

FORGOTTEN BY PEOPLE, ENGRAVED BY GOD

Can a mother forget her nursing child? Can she feel no love for the child she has borne? But even if that were possible, I would not forget you! See, I have written your name on the palms of my hands.

ISAIAH 49:15-16

I'll never forget as a senior in high school, walking into my guidance counselor's office full of dreams and excitement. I was ready to lay out my plan to play college basketball at my dream school. As I shared my vision, my counselor looked at me with a dismissive grin and said, "Caleb, I don't want to be the one to say this, but you will never play college basketball." I was stunned. His words pierced me. Outside of being a guidance counselor, he also coached college football, so I thought he must know what it takes. I left his office feeling defeated, misunderstood, and underestimated.

Maybe you've had a similar moment. A time when someone dismissed you, forgot you, or made you feel small. Like your dream was just a joke. Despite the rejection I felt that day, deep down, I believed God had placed that desire in my heart. And knowing this, I knew He must have a purpose for it. So I chose truth and hard work over doubt and disbelief. I pushed myself to become the best player I could be. At the end of my senior year, I didn't get a scholarship to my dream school. I went to junior college first. But two years later, I did earn that scholarship. And I'll never forget the satisfaction of walking around campus wearing my basketball gear, knowing those words spoken over me in my guidance counselor's office didn't define me.

If you're in a season of doubt—waiting for a spouse, a job, an opportunity—remember this: Being rejected or dismissed doesn't mean you're forgotten. God has written your name on His hands. His plan is good, and His timing is perfect.

Dear heavenly Father, *today I choose to trust Your Word over my own feelings. I believe You have a good plan for my life, and I choose to walk in that truth. I also pray for my future wife. Strengthen her mind and heart against the lies of the enemy. Protect her from discouragement, toxic thoughts, and the pain of being dismissed.*

When people forget her or treat her poorly, cover her with Your grace. Help her respond with truth and love. Show her how to shine Your light even in her struggles. Give her perseverance to endure trials, and replace every lie with Your truth. Let Your Word be the foundation she stands on, no matter what comes her way. Remind her daily that her name is engraved on the palms of Your hands and that You've prepared a purpose for her life. Guide both of us into that purpose in Your perfect timing. In Jesus' name, amen.

Love in Action . . .

Memorize Isaiah 49:16: "See, I have engraved you on the palms of my hands" (NIV). When you feel overlooked by others, remind yourself that you're never forgotten by God.

God never forgets His children.

WEEK

7

CONTENTMENT IS STRENGTH

True godliness with contentment is itself great wealth.

1 TIMOTHY 6:6

When I was growing up, my parents both worked at a Christian high school. I always loved tagging along to sporting events and school activities. It was such a fun environment, being around high school kids. The only drawback was that my parents didn't make much money. Even so, they had a way of making life joyful for my siblings and me.

One of my favorite memories was our monthly trip to Taco Bell. We'd get so excited to pick out whatever we wanted. To this day, I remember my order: two soft tacos with no lettuce, two nachos with cheese, and a small Dr Pepper, which I refilled as many times as I wanted. I'd wait at the counter, eager to receive my food, and then I would devour it as soon as I sat down. But the best part came after my meal: If we finished our food, my dad would give us each a dollar for cinnamon twists. That little treat sometimes felt like the greatest prize.

As a kid, I never thought about what we lacked. My parents were so good at helping us enjoy what we did have, making simple experiences fun and meaningful. That lesson of contentment has stuck with me. Contentment isn't based on receiving what you lack; it's based on gratitude for what God has already given you. Seasons change, and you'll never have the same one twice. Enjoy where you are now. Choose joy, thank God for His blessings, and let Him show you the good He's unveiling. When we learn contentment, our eyes turn back to the One who gives us all we need.

Dear God, *thank You for the blessings in my life and for always providing what I need. Today, I lift up my future wife to You. Sustain her in this season, and help her see the gifts You've placed all around her. Guard her from comparison, and point her back to Your truth when envy or discouragement takes hold. Protect her from the lies of the enemy that tempt her to compare her body, her purpose, or her possessions with others.*

Cover her with grace in moments when she feels like she's not enough, and remind her that she is fully loved by You. Ground her faith so she always runs to You first. Prepare both of us to build our marriage on gratitude and contentment, and shape us to fix our eyes on Jesus. In Your perfect timing, bring us together in marriage, ready to live with joy and contentment in You. In Jesus' name, amen.

Love in Action . . .

Tonight, write down three things you're grateful for in this season. Gratitude trains your heart to be steady instead of restless.

Contentment is turning our hearts toward Jesus, the Giver of all good things.

Father, thank You
for the ways You
are protecting me
and my future wife.

WEEK

8

REJECTION DOESN'T DEFINE YOU

The stone that the builders rejected has now become the cornerstone.

PSALM 118:22

After college, I had my sights set on a teaching job at my old high school. I had finished grad school and been subbing and coaching at the high school already. So when a position to teach history became available, I was first in line to apply. I asked some of the teachers if they thought I had a chance and was given the seal of approval by many. A few even thought I was a shoo-in for the job.

I went into the interview prepared and thought that I had completely knocked it out of the park. Considering my basketball dreams had been shattered in college, this felt like new purpose, a door that God was opening and something I could finally look forward to. That is, until I got my callback. I went into the principal's office expecting an offer, but what I got was a number of ways I was perfect for the job, but ultimately, they had decided to go with another candidate. I was devastated and disappointed. Old wounds came crashing down on me like a waterfall. *You're not good enough. God doesn't care about you. You should never go after your dreams.*

That rejection was tough to walk through, but years of separation have shown me that God had a much bigger plan.

One that I may have missed if I had gotten that job. My wife, Stefanie, often reminds me, "Rejection is often God's protection." Looking back now, I can see that's true. God was protecting me from something that wasn't His best and preparing me to receive something greater, something I could fully appreciate and steward well. If you're in a season of rejection, let me encourage you with this: Grieve the loss, place it at His feet, and trust that He's protecting you. Your story isn't over, and the best is yet to come.

Dear heavenly Father, *cover my future wife with Your love today. When she faces rejection, help her see it as Your protection. Remind her that You have a plan far better than anything she could imagine. Draw her close to You and hide her under the shadow of Your wings. Surround her with people who speak life, hope, and truth into her, and who point her back to You. Show her that rejection never determines her worth; she is chosen, loved, and created by You for a purpose. Give her wisdom to discern Your will in her choices and courage to walk the path You've planned for her.*

Do the same in me, Lord. Help me to trust You in seasons of rejection and to cling to Your truth over my every doubt. Prepare both of us in this season, and in Your perfect timing, bring us together with You as our foundation. In Jesus' name, amen.

Love in Action . . .

Read John 15:16 and then write the verse on a card: "You did not choose me, but I chose you and appointed you . . ." (NIV). Whenever a memory of rejection surfaces, read this verse aloud and remind yourself that you are always chosen by God.

Rejection is often God's protection.

WEEK

9 STOP COMPARING—RUN YOUR RACE

Oh, don't worry; we wouldn't dare say that we are as wonderful as these other men who tell you how important they are! But they are only comparing themselves with each other, using themselves as the standard of measurement. How ignorant!

2 CORINTHIANS 10:12

Social media can be a dangerous trap for comparison. Every day, highlight reels of other people's lives flash across your screen, and before long, you start to feel like your life doesn't measure up. You see a friend's new car, a baby announcement, or an extravagant proposal and think, *Why not me?*

Friend, what you allow into your life matters. Your story isn't the same as someone else's, and that's a good thing. But the enemy wants you to forget that. His tactic is the same as it was in the garden of Eden, tempting Adam and Eve to doubt God's goodness by promising them something "better."

Comparison only robs your peace. That's why boundaries are so important. For Stefanie and me, one change we made in our marriage was to stop looking at our phones first thing in the morning or late at night in bed. Instead, we choose to go to God first and last each day. We were tired of the wasted time scrolling, which only left us feeling restless.

Setting boundaries changed everything. Who you follow, what you watch, and when you watch it matters. I've found so much more peace when I go to God's Word first thing in the morning. When I start the day with His truth, I can operate from the Spirit instead of the flesh. Your story is unique, designed by God Himself. Stop looking to the right or the left. Fix your eyes on Jesus, and He will establish your steps.

Dear God, *help my future wife fix her eyes on You today. Protect her from comparison, which steals joy. Open her eyes to the blessings You've already placed in her life, and give her a heart of gratitude. Guard her thoughts, her eyes, and her heart. Give her wisdom to set healthy boundaries around the content she consumes and the people she gives access to her life. Surround her with a community that uplifts her, prays for her, and points her back to You. Remove anything, or anyone, that would distract her from growing in You.*

Guide her daily into Your purpose, keeping her eyes on the prize of Christ. Cover her with love and grace as she interacts with others, and help her to see people through Your eyes. Do the same for me, Lord. Protect me from comparison, and keep my heart fixed on Your calling. Lead both of us toward each other in Your perfect timing, and give us strength to wait well. In Jesus' name, amen.

Love in Action . . .

Delete or mute one social media account today that stirs up comparison in your heart. Replace that time with reading Proverbs 4:25-27, which encourages us to stay on our own path.

Comparison kills progress.
Run your own race.

WEEK

10

FORGIVENESS IS POWER

Make allowance for each other's faults, and forgive anyone who offends you. Remember, the Lord forgave you, so you must forgive others.

COLOSSIANS 3:13

One of my biggest regrets in marriage came during a season when I pushed past my wife's wisdom and instead decided to pursue an opportunity for our business. Stefanie and I are relationship mentors who help singles looking to get married and married couples who want to have thriving marriages through coaching, resources, and books. Because of our large audience and encouraging content, we had been noticed by a prominent ministry and were approached to work full-time for them doing exactly what we were already doing. I was all in. I thought it would bring us financial stability, give us more free time, and open doors to a bigger stage in ministry. Stefanie, on the other hand, had serious reservations. But instead of slowing down and truly listening to her concerns, I bulldozed her opinions and pushed us forward anyway. In the end, the business opportunity didn't work out, and the fallout was huge—financially, emotionally, and relationally in our marriage.

What hurt the most was realizing how much I had broken Stefanie's trust. Picking up the pieces meant apologizing, listening to her heart, and owning the fact that I hadn't valued her voice in a decision we should have made together. It took time, but thankfully, I have a forgiving wife. Slowly, God rebuilt her trust in me. Through it all, I learned this: Forgiveness is power. It frees us from the chains of pain, bad decisions, and brokenness, and it moves us toward wholeness with others and God. Watching Him heal our marriage through this situation has been both humbling and beautiful.

Now, Stefanie and I are resolute in our decision-making. If we don't feel God's peace about something, we don't move forward. Unity matters. Forgiveness matters. And God uses both for His glory.

Heavenly Father, *I pray for protection over my future wife today. When people or situations hurt her, give her the strength to walk in forgiveness. Remind her that forgiveness doesn't erase the pain but frees her from resentment and bitterness. Pour out Your grace on her so she can handle every situation with peace. If there's any unforgiveness in her heart, help her release it to You. Cover her with Your truth and goodness as she grows in this powerful discipline, preparing her heart for a marriage where forgiveness brings unity, not division.*

Do the same in me, Lord. Teach me to forgive as You have forgiven me. Help me release every hurt, every wrong, and every disappointment so I can walk in the freedom You've already given. Renew my future wife each day with Your love that covers all things. Let forgiveness be the rhythm of our hearts and the strength of our future marriage. In Jesus' name, amen.

Love in Action . . .

Think of one person who has hurt you in the past. Out loud, say, "I release you to God." Forgiveness is a man's strength, not his weakness.

Strong men choose forgiveness.

WEEK

11

OWN IT: CONVICTION AND CONFESSION

People who conceal their sins will not prosper, but if they confess and turn from them, they will receive mercy.

PROVERBS 28:13

There was someone in my life, let's call him Roger, who really knew how to get under my skin. The things he said and the way he treated people would immediately irritate me. I wouldn't say anything to his face, but when I got home, I'd unload on Stefanie or friends, slandering him and tearing him down, convincing myself I was better because *I'd never act like that.*

The problem was, I was so focused on pointing out Roger's faults that I ignored my own sin, anger, pride, and judgment. My bitterness was starting to spill over into my other relationships, even my marriage. Stefanie agreed Roger's behavior was wrong, but she didn't agree with how I was handling it. She was right. One day, God convicted me. I needed to stop hiding behind my frustration and actually confess my own sin, anger, slander, and judgment. I resisted at first, but when I finally repented and released my sin to Him, it felt like a massive weight lifted off my shoulders.

I've been on a journey since then of learning to see Roger through Jesus' eyes. The more I confess and let go, the more I see a person who's hurting and in need of God's love, just like me. Secret sin always grows in the dark. It can warp our thoughts and actions until we're not walking in the fruit of the Spirit. I'm thankful God convicted me to own it, confess it, and find peace in Him. That's the power of repentance; it frees us to love like Jesus.

Dear God, *I pray over my future wife today. Cover her with Your love and grace. If there are things she's carrying that she hasn't brought before You, convict her gently and show her that true freedom comes through repentance and oneness with You. Break any chains that are weighing her down and keeping her from fully experiencing Your joy. Show her practical ways to lay those burdens before You in prayer.*

Do the same in me, Lord. Reveal any hidden sin, lead me through confession, and lead me into Your freedom. Help us both walk into the future You have for us without the baggage of unconfessed sin. May our lives be marked by mercy, honesty, and peace. In Jesus' name, amen.

Love in Action . . .

Open your Bible to 1 John 1:9. Out loud, confess one sin before God and pray, "Lord, I repent and receive Your cleansing." Kneel when you pray to physically posture your body in humility before Him.

Confession is the doorway to holiness.

WEEK

12

NO CONDEMNATION, NO CHAINS

If the Son sets you free, you are truly free.

JOHN 8:36

In my adolescent years, I was sexually abused by an extended family member. That experience left me with deep wounds, low self-worth, guilt, and a belief that I wasn't worthy of real love. To cope, I turned to pornography to feel some sense of control over my emotions. What started as a crutch became an addiction that lasted more than a decade. By God's grace, He helped me break free from pornography once and for all.

Even still, I carried shame. That shame caused me to withdraw and look for escape in other places, like video games. Eventually, I realized that my healing wouldn't come from my own strength. I needed to hand over my sins, my pain, and my past to Jesus. When I invited Him into those dark places, He met me with compassion and began to heal me. I clung to the truth of Romans 8:1: "There is no condemnation for those who belong to Christ Jesus." Slowly, God set me free, not only from my behavior, but also from the guilt and shame that chained me down.

Today, I walk in freedom. I've forgiven the family member who hurt me, and I've received healing from the abuse I endured. I don't know what your past holds, but don't let it rob you of the future God has for you. Lay it all at His feet. His love is stronger than your shame. His forgiveness is greater than your failures. You don't have to stay chained to your past; you can walk freely into the future He has for you.

Heavenly Father, *I lift up my future wife to You today. Comfort her where she needs comfort, and encourage her in her weaknesses. Reveal anything she needs to place in Your hands, whether it's sin, unforgiveness, pain, resentment, or anger. Remind her that her past does not define her, and her identity is secure in Christ. Heal her from shame and guilt and the wounds she carries. Let her experience the freedom You promise, walking boldly into her future without the chains of her past. Your Word says there is no condemnation for those who are in Christ Jesus.*

Do the same in me, Lord. Break me free of any chains that hold me back, and give me the courage to lay everything in Your hands. Prepare us both to enter marriage with freedom, healing, and hope, ready for the future You've designed. In Jesus' name, amen.

Love in Action . . .

Write Romans 8:1 on a note card: "There is no condemnation for those who belong to Christ Jesus." Place it in your Bible, and read it whenever feelings of shame creep in.

Shame has no place where Christ reigns.

WEEK

13 IT'S THE THOUGHT THAT COUNTS

Let all that you do be done in love.

1 CORINTHIANS 16:14, ESV

In marriage, it's important to keep dating your spouse and go out of your way to be romantic. Setting the mood on a romantic date can make a big difference.

Early on in our marriage, I decided to surprise Stefanie with a date night on our porch. I set up the patio furniture, brought out a TV, prepared some snacks, and even lit some tiki torches to create the perfect atmosphere. I told Stefanie to wait upstairs until everything was ready. The last step was pouring some beverages. When I stepped back inside to grab our drinks, I noticed our house suddenly looked a lot brighter than before. I turned around in horror to see one of our patio chairs completely engulfed in six-foot flames that nearly reached our upper porch. I yelled in disbelief and sprinted for water. Stefanie rushed downstairs, saw the fire, broke open the fire extinguisher case, and handed it to me. Within seconds, the flames were out. Thankfully, only the chair was damaged, but my dream of a romantic evening turned into cleanup duty. We laughed about it later, and to this day, I still avoid anything that involves fire on dates.

There is a timeless cliché that says, "It's the thought that counts," and I truly believe in that statement. The more intentional that you are in your relationships, the deeper you can go, and intimacy thrives. One thing I've learned through dating and marriage is that *thoughtfulness is underrated.* Learn to be thoughtful. Learn to go the extra mile. Being intentional lets the other person know you're thinking of her and that you *want* to be a blessing.

Whatever season you're in, whether you're dating, single, or married, take time to show love in the small things. For all the times I've messed up while trying to be thoughtful, Stefanie has never once complained that I was doing something kind for her. It's always been appreciated, and those moments have made a lasting difference in our marriage.

Dear God, *thank You for the way You love me with such intentionality and care. Teach me to slow down and notice the people You've placed in my life. Help me to be thoughtful in the way I speak, give, listen, and show love. I lift up my future wife to You today. Guide her closer to You, and help her to see the blessings around her. Help others do thoughtful things for her each day so she can feel loved and appreciated. Cultivate in her an intentional spirit where she shows her appreciation for others.*

I pray that we would take time in our future marriage to be intentional with each other, noting ways we can bless each other and coming up with thoughtful ways to surprise each other.

When I'm tempted to rush or overlook the small things, remind me that simple acts of kindness can carry eternal impact. Fill my heart with creativity and compassion so that my thoughtfulness reflects Your heart. May everything I do be done in love and bring joy to those around me. In Jesus' name, amen.

Love in Action . . .

Look for one intentional way to show thoughtfulness today to someone in your life, through a message, a prayer, or a small act of kindness. Practice being the kind of person who notices and serves with love, even in the little things.

Thoughtfulness is love in action.

Father, give her wisdom
to discern Your will
in her choices and courage
to walk the path You've
planned for her.

WEEK

14 LEARNING PATIENCE AND TRUST IN THE UNKNOWN

The LORD is good to those who wait for him, to the soul who seeks him.

LAMENTATIONS 3:25, ESV

I'll never forget the day I first laid eyes on Stefanie. I walked into church one Sunday, and as I entered the sanctuary, I looked to my left. There, worshiping about three rows from the front, was Stefanie. She was pouring out her heart to the Lord in the most beautiful way. I often tell people that I saw her heavenly spirit that day. I was smitten on the spot and knew I needed to get to know that girl. After the service ended, I headed over to the young adults hangout across the street from the church, where there was live music, a coffee bar, and time to connect with friends and new acquaintances. I was hoping and praying she would be over there.

I spotted Stefanie right away and built up the courage to walk over and talk to her. After I introduced myself, another guy walked over, gave me a dirty look, and put his arm around Stefanie. It was like he was a Spanish conquistador claiming his territory. I respectfully said my goodbyes and walked away.

Thankfully, I was at a point in my singleness where I was putting my full trust in God. I decided to leave her in His hands in that moment and in the year that followed. I would daily tell people about the "dream girl" at church, but I would release her over to God in my prayers, knowing that if we were meant to be together, He would make it happen. After a year had passed and her relationship had ended, I was able to make my move. God often has a bigger and better plan than ours. And as we choose to trust Him with our lives, He is faithful and will come through in ways we can't even imagine. The fact that Stefanie is now my wife is a constant reminder of His faithfulness.

Dear heavenly Father, *thank You for knowing the deepest desires of my heart and for writing a story far greater than anything I could plan. I lift up my future wife to You today. Guide her and shape her in her waiting seasons of life. Show her that Your plans are greater and that this waiting is not for nothing.*

Teach me to trust You fully, Lord. Help me to release what I long for into Your hands and to rest in Your timing. When it's right, You'll make it clear. When it's not, You'll give me peace to wait. Prepare my heart to love like You, patiently, purely, and with faith that You're working behind the scenes. Thank You that no delay is wasted and no prayer goes unheard. I trust that You'll bring the right person into my life at the right time, in Your perfect way. In Jesus' name, amen.

Love in Action . . .

Think of the person or desire you've been holding on to tightly. Take a moment to pray, "God, I release this into Your hands. If it's Your will, bring this back in Your perfect timing. Until then, help me trust You with peace and patience."

If what I long for is from God, I don't have to force it. His timing will make it happen.

WEEK

15

BREAKING CYCLES, BUILDING A LEGACY

Understand, therefore, that the Lord *your God is indeed God. He is the faithful God who keeps his covenant for a thousand generations and lavishes his unfailing love on those who love him and obey his commands.*

DEUTERONOMY 7:9

Growing up, I was always different from my two brothers. I was athletic, more outgoing, and not as interested in school. My brothers, on the other hand, excelled in academics and today are some of the most intelligent people I know. They are more quiet and reserved, and they both love science and world history. As kids, however, we did not always get along. If my brothers got into trouble, they'd pin it on me, knowing I'd fight back and end up looking more guilty.

Over time, this cycle made me defensive—a reflex I carried into adulthood and into marriage. As you might imagine, this led to many long nights and arguments with Stefanie early in our marriage. I had a hard time acknowledging when I was wrong, especially when I *felt* I wasn't, and it cost us our sense of peace and connection. Through our prayers, intentional work, and trust-building, however, God began to break my defensive walls down. I had to lay my pride down and consider how my actions impacted Stefanie's feelings and heart. Listening with a loving ear, instead of a defensive one, has changed everything.

Looking back, I wish I had started working on this when I was single. It would have spared Stefanie unnecessary pain and made her feel more loved earlier in our marriage. Perhaps you can relate. I encourage you to ask, *What cycles or patterns do I need to deal with now before marriage?* Healing from negative patterns in this season will save you pain, arguments, and broken trust later.

Dear God, *thank You for my future wife. I pray that You would break any negative cycles in her life. Give her wisdom and strategy to replace lies with Your truth. If she feels stuck, show her the way out through Your love and grace. Surround her with healthy community that brings healing and encouragement to her. Reveal any toxic family patterns she may be following, and help her break free from anything that would hinder her purpose.*

Do the same work in me, Lord. Heal the patterns in my life that don't honor You, and replace them with habits that bring peace and love. Prepare us both for marriage by creating healthy rhythms in our hearts. Lead us into freedom and unity, and in Your perfect timing, bring us together in marriage, ready to build a legacy rooted in Your truth. In Jesus' name, amen.

Love in Action . . .

Stand up and say out loud, “In Jesus’ name, the negative cycles of my family end with me. I will build a new legacy of faithfulness and strength.”

With God’s power, I can end toxic cycles and build a godly legacy.

WEEK

16

INTEGRITY IS WHO YOU ARE WHEN NO ONE IS LOOKING

Finally, brothers and sisters, whatever is true, whatever is noble, whatever is right, whatever is pure, whatever is lovely, whatever is admirable—if anything is excellent or praiseworthy—think about such things.

PHILIPPIANS 4:8, NIV

Integrity is built in the everyday moments of life. It's often in the small choices, when no one is watching. I enjoy doing the grocery shopping, and sometimes I'll have a cart packed full of food for the next week or two. Since Stefanie and I eat a lot of fresh, organic items, there's always plenty to go through at checkout. On several occasions, I have paid, walked out to the car, unloaded my items, and realized I forgot to scan the case of water sitting on the bottom rack of my cart. In those moments, I have a choice to make. It would be easy to shrug off a case of water and think, *It's not much money. They won't even notice.* But integrity is about choosing what honors God, even when it costs you something.

Any time something like this has happened, I've made the decision to go back inside and pay for the forgotten item. Honestly, the cashier is sometimes surprised that I bothered. But for me, it's about knowing I did the right thing before God, respecting the store, and being an honest man. Integrity isn't forged in dramatic, high-stakes moments. It's shaped in the small, unseen ones, where it would be easy to compromise. That's where the battle line is drawn, between convenience and conviction. When you choose integrity in the small things, you're preparing yourself for the bigger tests ahead—in your relationships, in your marriage, and in every part of life.

Dear God, *I lift up my future wife to You today. Draw her close to You, and shape her into a woman of integrity, honesty, and truth. Show her the areas where she needs to grow, and give her the courage to choose what is right even when it's not easy. Help us both to be intentional in this season, working on the qualities we long to see in each other so that we may honor You in marriage. Guard us from laziness and bad habits, and teach us to live faithfully, even in the small, unseen moments. Prepare us to be spouses who point each other closer to You and the specific call You've placed on our lives. In Jesus' name, amen.*

Love in Action . . .

Think of a man in your life who displays integrity. In a journal, write down the characteristics he displays that you would like to emulate.

The man I am in private is the man I'll be in marriage.

WEEK

17

WINNING THE BATTLE FOR PURITY

I made a covenant with my eyes not to look with lust at a young woman.

JOB 31:1

The Bible teaches that our eyes are like the lamp of our body and that what we choose to focus on fills our heart with either light or darkness. In today's world, with screens everywhere, it's nearly impossible not to be faced with temptation. That's why purity requires intentionality. One way I've chosen to fight temptation is by giving Stefanie full access to my phone, at any time and for any reason. I have nothing to hide, and that accountability helps me to stay vigilant. My peace with her is far more important than my pride.

As a relationship coach, I see the topic of purity come up a lot with my male clients. I often tell them to use this filter: *Would you be comfortable watching certain content with your wife next to you?* Even better, *Would you watch that content if Jesus was sitting beside you?* If the answer is no, then it doesn't belong in your feed or on your screen. This isn't about shame; it's about living freely. Purity isn't something you lose; it's something you protect and strengthen.

Over time, I've found that when you cut off sources of temptation, the urges you've had begin to fade, and walking in purity becomes easier. This is a battle, and the enemy will do everything he can to trip you up. But when you set boundaries and guard your eyes, you're not just avoiding sin; you're inviting God to transform your heart. Choose today to fight for purity. It's worth it for your life now, and it's worth it for your future marriage.

Heavenly Father, *I pray protection over my future wife's eyes, mind, and heart. Guard her from anything impure, lustful, or harmful that would compromise her values. Keep her away from influences, online or in person, that would tempt her to step outside Your will. Help her to see purity as a gift, something beautiful to be pursued and protected. Teach her to set healthy boundaries that will keep her strong in moments of temptation.*

Lord, cover us both with grace when we stumble. Break away shame and guilt, and replace them with the light of Your love. Prepare us to fight for purity now so that our future marriage will be built on trust, faithfulness, and Your truth. Amen.

Love in Action . . .

Before you begin each day, pray, “Lord, guard my eyes and my heart.” End each day with a clear mind.

Purity today is faithfulness tomorrow.

WEEK

18

CONFIDENCE ROOTED IN CHRIST

Blessed are those who trust in the Lord *and have made the* Lord *their hope and confidence.*
JEREMIAH 17:7

Where do you find your confidence? In a hard day's work? In praise from your peers? In your accomplishments? Or do you find your confidence in Christ? When I injured my back and lost the chance to pursue my dream of playing professional basketball, I struggled with confidence for years. My injury slammed the door on my dream, and I began to believe the negative thoughts that circled through my mind: *I'm not good enough. I can't do anything else well.* Those lies crushed my confidence, led me to settle for less than God's best, and allowed bad habits to creep deeper into my life.

What eventually helped me overcome it? Speaking truth over my life. I caught the lies when they surfaced, and I replaced them with God's promises: *I am God's child. God has a good purpose for my life. I can do all things through Christ who strengthens me.* The more I spoke these truths, the more I believed them. Confidence doesn't come from applause, achievements, or other people's approval. It comes from God. The Bible says you are His masterpiece, created with purpose and value. When you fix your eyes on Jesus, He establishes your steps and gives you the confidence to walk in them. If you wrestle with insecurity, or even pride, bring it to Him. He will heal what's broken, humble what's inflated, and anchor your confidence in His truth. Your past doesn't define you. Your Creator does.

Dear God, *I lift up my future wife to You today. Remind her that she is beautifully and wonderfully made, created with a unique purpose only she can fulfill. Surround her with people who speak life and truth over her and push her toward growth, fruitfulness, and faithfulness. Expose any lies she believes about herself, and replace them with Your Word. Let her confidence rest in being Your beloved child, deeply loved and fully accepted. Provide for her in this season so she never doubts her worth.*

Do the same in me, Lord. Heal my insecurities, silence any lies I believe about my identity or future, and prepare me to be a husband who builds my wife up and points her to You. In the mighty name of Jesus, amen.

Love in Action . . .

Look in the mirror and declare three truths from Scripture about who you are in Christ: chosen, forgiven, equipped. Let His Word speak louder than your insecurities.

Real confidence is built on Christ, not compliments.

WEEK

19

REAL LEADERS SERVE FIRST

But among you it will be different. Those who are the greatest among you should take the lowest rank, and the leader should be like a servant.

LUKE 22:26

One of my favorite parts of being married is serving and loving my wife in practical ways. If Stefanie tells me something she needs, I do whatever I can to make it happen. One of her passions is healthy living. In the mornings, she has several different drinks: an electrolyte mix, celery juice, hot pepper and fruit juice, aloe juice, and sometimes tea. I noticed that making all of these took her time and slowed down the start of her day. So one morning, I decided to make them for her. Immediately, I could tell a burden was lifted from her shoulders. More than that, the simple act of service made her feel loved, seen, and appreciated.

I never thought I'd be the kind of guy who cared about juicing or preparing morning drinks. But I've always wanted to be a leader, and real leadership starts with service. Yes, serving my wife may add a little extra time to my mornings, but it adds so much more to my life. It strengthens our marriage, builds trust, makes my wife feel loved, and reminds me that leadership is about lowering yourself to lift others up.

Serving others doesn't have to be anything grand or complicated. Start small. Do one thing today to bless someone else. As you build the habit of serving and being thoughtful now, you're laying the foundation for a future marriage filled with peace, joy, and mutual love.

Heavenly Father, *I pray for my future wife today. Open her heart to causes, missions, or people she can serve. Surround her with a strong church community, where she can use her gifts to further Your Kingdom. Give her eyes to see the needs around her and wisdom to know how to meet them. Fill her with joy as she serves and teach her to set healthy boundaries so she doesn't burn out. Provide people who will pour back into her as she pours into others.*

Do the same in me, Lord. Teach me to lead by serving, both now and in my marriage. Thank You for giving us opportunities to love and serve others the way Jesus served us. In Jesus' name, amen.

Love in Action . . .

Do one act of service today without telling anyone. Take out the trash, help a neighbor, or cover for a teammate. Becoming a leader starts with serving others.

True strength looks like Jesus—serving first, loving most, and leading with humility.

Father, prepare us to fight for purity now so that our future marriage will be built on trust, faithfulness, and Your truth.

WEEK

20

MONEY, MISSION, AND MARRIAGE PREP

Wealth from get-rich-quick schemes quickly disappears; wealth from hard work grows over time.

PROVERBS 13:11

I have so much respect for my wife. One of the bravest things she ever did was pack her car with everything she owned, drive across the country, and move to Pasadena, California, a city where she didn't know a single person, to pursue her master's degree in marriage and family therapy. She had saved for years, a discipline she learned from her own family, and built a small nest egg to live on during school. Her housing wasn't glamorous. It was a small corner room with almost no natural light, a futon that doubled as her bed, and a window that faced the outside dumpster. But instead of complaining, she was grateful.

When we started dating, I was struck by how she had made that little space feel like home. As our relationship grew more serious, she shared how expensive her rent had become. I had just started a new job, and while my budget was tight, I decided to help her each month simply to bless her. Supporting her in that season not only gave her stability but also prepared us for the future. After she completed her degree, we were even able to live in that same apartment during our first year of marriage.

Stefanie's faithfulness in following God's call, saving diligently, and being resourceful showed me what it looks like to trust God with money. Over the years, we've combined our strengths to build a solid foundation for our family. Likewise, the best thing you can do now is to take small, faithful steps with what you have. When you trust God with your resources, He blesses you in ways you could never predict.

Heavenly Father, *I lift up my future wife's finances to You. Give her wisdom to steward her resources well and to use them for Your glory. Provide steady work and opportunities that meet her needs and allow her to prepare for the future. Surround her with wise mentors who will guide her with grace. Instill in her a generous heart toward the church and others, and protect her from fear, stress, or worry about money.*

Likewise, Lord, shape me into a strong leader in this area, humble enough to learn, disciplined enough to grow, and wise enough to seek counsel when needed. Help us both to build habits now that will prepare us for peace and stability in our marriage. In Jesus' name, amen.

Love in Action . . .

Bring God into your spending. Before your next purchase, stop and pray, asking the Lord if your purchase is wise.

A man who manages money well builds a strong home.

WEEK

21

LIVING ON PURPOSE NOW

My life is worth nothing to me unless I use it for finishing the work assigned me by the Lord Jesus—the work of telling others the Good News about the wonderful grace of God.

ACTS 20:24

Waiting seasons can make you feel like you're standing still. It's easy to slip into the mindset of "when my life starts," "when God answers this prayer," or "when I'm finally with the right person." But purpose doesn't begin when your circumstances line up. Purpose begins now. God shapes us while we walk, not while we sit.

There was a season before I met Stefanie when I realized I had a choice: I could sit in discouragement, or I could start becoming the man I wanted to be. I knew I had always wanted to make an impact on the world, so when the opportunity came to go on a mission trip to Nicaragua with the school I worked at, I said yes. I ended up going twice over two years, and those trips changed me.

We spent our days at a facility that gave local kids a safe place to play sports, laugh, and be surrounded by community. I watched our students pour out love on the kids, and I watched the kids respond with joy and trust. We cleaned out the baseball dugout, painted a mural, made improvements to the basketball court, and helped in several other ways. I remember thinking, *This is the kind of man I want to be: someone who shows up, serves, and invests in people.* That experience grew my confidence, stretched my faith, and helped me discover parts of my purpose long before I knew who I would marry.

Looking back, I'm grateful I didn't wait for life to "start" before stepping into something meaningful. Those trips didn't just impact the kids we served; they shaped me into the husband I would eventually become.

Don't wait to start living. Start now. Go on that trip. Learn a new skill. Get healthier. Step into community. Take a step of faith toward the dream God put on your heart. Most of all, trust Him with your whole heart. When you live with purpose in this season, God will use it to prepare you for the next.

Dear God, *I lift up my future wife to You today. Give her purpose in this season. Turn her pain into promise, and guide her to walk boldly in what You've called her to do. When discouragement comes, surround her with people who will build her up and point her back to Your truth. Provide what she needs to pursue her calling wholeheartedly. Show her any lies or limiting beliefs she may be holding on to and replace them with Your promises.*

Do the same for me, Lord. Grow me in confidence and purpose. Surround me with good community, and keep me faithful to the dream You've placed on my heart. Help us both to keep pressing on toward the prize of Christ Jesus, never giving up. And in Your perfect timing, lead us to each other. In Jesus' name, amen.

Love in Action . . .

Take fifteen minutes to work on one project, dream, or skill God has placed on your heart. Purpose grows when you move toward it, not when you wait.

**Purpose isn't found someday;
it's built today.**

WEEK

22

IDENTITY FIRST, MARRIAGE SECOND

You are not like that, for you are a chosen people. You are royal priests, a holy nation, God's very own possession.

1 PETER 2:9

Before I met Stefanie, I was convinced that marriage would solve all my problems. I thought, *I'll finally be intimate with a woman. I'll never be lonely, and I'll always have someone by my side.* The problem, however, was that none of these thoughts involved God.

Friend, we aren't meant to find peace, purpose, or fulfillment in another person. Only God can provide those things. In my singleness, God had to teach me to find my worth and identity in Him alone. I remember pleading with God for a wife. Looking back, though, I realize how unhealthy a marriage would have been for me at the time. I was a shell of a person, not anywhere near who He made me to be, and most important, I was not fully rooted in Him.

Finding my identity in God didn't just help me endure a hard season; it healed me and prepared me for the right person. God brought me someone who would challenge me, love me, and always point me back to Him. Marriage is a gift, but it was never meant to be an idol. When we put it above God, we miss the point. Place Him first in your life. Let Him be the desire of your heart.

Dear God, *prepare my future wife's heart for the work You want to do in her life and in our future marriage. Encourage her in her gifts, and prompt her in the areas where she needs to grow. Surround her with people who will point her toward You, who will speak truth with honesty and love, and who will remind her of who she is in Christ.*

I pray that our marriage would honor You and that everything we do together would be for Your glory. Stir in us a vision for how we can serve, whether through ministry, community, or being a light in our family. Give us both courage to seek You first and to shine Your light daily. Show us the path You've laid out for us, and in Your perfect timing, bring us together in marriage. In Jesus' name, amen.

Love in Action . . .

Today, spend intentional time with God. Open His Word, talk to Him about your desires, and ask for His wisdom to guide your steps. Let your relationship with Him be your greatest pursuit, trusting that everything else, including marriage, flows from that place.

Place your identity first and foremost in Christ before anything else.

WEEK

23

MARRIAGE: A LIVING PICTURE OF CHRIST

I am jealous for you with the jealousy of God himself. I promised you as a pure bride to one husband—Christ.

2 CORINTHIANS 11:2

One of the wildest stories I've heard come out of our online ministry was from a woman in Europe who reached out to me. She told me that simply by watching how I loved my wife on Instagram, she was led to believe in Jesus. I was floored. At first, I didn't even know how to respond. Social media is so full of noise, yet somehow, through the consistency of our marriage on display, God broke through and moved this woman's heart. She explained that it wasn't one single post, but what she noticed over time—how I loved Stefanie, how we interacted, and how we supported each other through both good and hard seasons. Those everyday moments of love and faithfulness eventually pointed her to her Creator, and she rededicated her life to Jesus.

That conversation has stayed with me. Whenever I start to lose perspective, I remind myself of her story. It's proof that marriage isn't just about two people being happy together; it's meant to be a living picture of something greater. Scripture reminds us that marriage is designed to reflect Christ's love for the church. Even in the face of rejection, opposition, and death itself, Jesus never stopped loving His people. He served, sacrificed, and gave His life so that we could live. Marriage is called to display that same kind of committed love. Not a perfect love—we're human, after all—but a steadfast love that points beyond ourselves and gives the world a glimpse of God's heart.

—

Dear heavenly Father, *my desire is to be married one day. Prepare my heart now so I can love my future wife the way Christ loves the church. Grow in me a steadfast spirit, a patient heart, and a love that is kind and sacrificial. Show me the ways I still need to grow so I can be the husband my future wife deserves.*

I pray for her as well. Strengthen her in her walk with You. Help her to release any pain she carries from her past or present so she can live wholeheartedly before You. May our future marriage reflect Your love and be a living picture of Christ and the church. Prepare us in every way we need, and open our hearts to receive all You have for us in this season and the next. In Jesus' name, amen.

Love in Action . . .

Think about God's love for you, how patient, forgiving, and unconditional it is. Let that love be your example as you grow. Ask yourself how you can reflect His character now, in your words, your choices, and the way you care for others, so that one day, your marriage will be built on that same kind of selfless love.

Marriage is a mirror of Christ's love.

Father, I pray that our marriage would honor You and that everything we do together would be for Your glory.

WEEK

24

COVENANT > CONTRACT

Since they are no longer two but one, let no one split apart what God has joined together.

MATTHEW 19:6

Being an entrepreneur has taught me the value of contracts. Having clear details, deliverables, and structure laid out makes it much easier to work with other businesses. I'll admit, I can be a stickler about contracts due to past experiences. Broken promises led to broken agreements, leaving me with the fallout. Those outcomes made trusting others really difficult.

So when I think about marriage, I can't imagine treating it like a contract. There would be countless addendums. And if one of us failed, would it all be over? That's no way to build a relationship. Thankfully, God calls us to something higher. Jesus said that when two people marry, they become one, and what God has joined together, no one should separate.

Marriage isn't a legal agreement; it's a covenant. And while marriage has been the greatest joy of my life, it hasn't been without its painful seasons. But even in those moments of loss, heartache, and disappointment, our greatest blessing has been running toward each other and pointing each other back to God. Sure, it might be easy to run away, blame, or let pride take over, but Scripture calls us to love differently. Ephesians 5:25 tells husbands to love their wives as Christ loved the church, sacrificially laying down His life, so that she may be holy and clean. Every day in marriage, we have that choice: to die to our pride, selfishness, and preconceived ideas, and to love our wife like Jesus. Marriage was never meant to be a contract. It's meant to be a covenant, a living picture of God's unconditional love.

Dear heavenly Father, *help me to walk with honesty and integrity in all my relationships. Give me courage to keep my word, even when it's difficult. Shape my future wife and me into people who are trustworthy and steadfast. When she feels like quitting, give her perseverance. When I feel pride rising up, teach me humility. Reveal to us the places where we need to grow in trusting You, and prepare us for a covenant marriage that reflects Your love. May we choose to fight for each other every day, even when it's hard. Fix our eyes on You as the foundation of our future marriage. In the mighty name of Jesus, amen.*

Love in Action . . .

Today, pray the following out loud: "Lord, make me a man who keeps his word even when it's hard. Prepare me to see marriage as a covenant, not a convenience."

Marriage is a covenant, not a contract I can walk away from.

WEEK

25

SELFLESSNESS IS STRENGTH

Don't look out only for your own interests, but take an interest in others, too.

PHILIPPIANS 2:4

Stefanie is the most selfless person I know. She does everything with others in mind and has this quiet way of showing people that they matter, which never fails to inspire me. One of her habits is writing thank-you notes. You might remember those handwritten letters of gratitude dropped in the mail. It's a long-lost art and honestly something I wish more people practiced, including myself. But Stefanie does it faithfully. Whenever someone does something kind for us, she takes the time to write a thoughtful letter and send it off. It's such a simple act, but it communicates her gratitude and affection for that person. On top of letters, she also loves surprising others with small gifts or flowers, sometimes delivered in person, other times sent right to their door. Those gestures may seem small, but they mean the world to the people receiving them.

Another thing I admire about Stefanie is how well she listens. She doesn't just wait for her turn to talk; she asks follow-up questions and makes the other person feel like the center of the conversation. These small but consistent acts of love have changed me. They're rare, and they're powerful. Watching how Stefanie loves others has shifted my own thoughts and behaviors. Because of her, I've grown into a more patient, attentive, and loving person. Her selflessness doesn't just bless others; it's transformed me too.

Dear God, *be with my future wife and help her to choose love, grace, and kindness in her actions. Show her the blessing that flows from living selflessly, and give her strength when she feels weary. Provide opportunities for her to serve others with her time, her gifts, and her presence. Bring ministries or communities to mind where she can pour out her strengths. Fill her cup as she pours out for others. Do the same work in me, Lord. Help me to die to myself and grow into the kind of husband who loves sacrificially, as Christ loved the church. Let pride have no place in our future marriage, but instead fill us both with the fruit of the Spirit. Lead us toward each other in Your perfect timing. In Jesus' name, amen.*

Love in Action . . .

Give up one comfort today for someone else: the better seat, the last word, the extra portion. Training in selflessness now makes you stronger later.

Selflessness is having the strength to consider others before yourself.

WEEK

26

GIVING GOD THE GLORY EVEN IN YOUR PAIN

Whether you eat or drink, or whatever you do, do it all for the glory of God.

1 CORINTHIANS 10:31

The hardest moment of my life was finding out about the passing of our twin baby boys, Asher and Shiloh. Becoming parents had been a dream of ours, and when Stefanie and I went in for our first ultrasound, we were overjoyed to hear the news—there was not just one baby, but twins. It felt like the greatest gift, a double blessing, answered prayers. But within ten minutes, everything changed. The doctor told us there were no heartbeats. In an instant, our greatest joy turned into our greatest heartbreak. The drive home was somber. We wept the whole way, mourning the loss of two precious lives we would never hold on this side of heaven. When we finally got home, it felt like the air had been sucked out of the room. Through tears, Stefanie turned to me and asked, "What do we do?" I had no answers. No way to fix it. No words to console her or even myself. The only words that came to mind were "We worship God." So right there in our living room, in the thick of our pain, we turned on worship music and began to sing, lifting our voices and acknowledging He was still King.

That moment marked me forever. It taught me that even in the darkest valleys, God is beside us, and we must turn to Him.

Marriage isn't about chasing happiness. It's about glorifying God together. And when we chose to worship Him instead of running from Him, God met us there and began the slow, holy work of healing our hearts.

—

Dear God, *I pray blessings over my future wife today. When she faces pain or disappointment, remind her that she's never alone. Help her release every burden into Your hands and find peace in Your presence. Help her to find joy in both the small and big moments of life. Be with her in her pain, and give her the courage to release it into Your hands. Marriage is about glorifying You, Father, in good times and in bad.*

Shape both of us in this season so our lives reflect Your love and truth. Prepare our hearts to glorify You through every high and low, knowing that marriage is first and foremost about honoring You. I pray our future marriage would be full of grace, sacrifice, and praise to You alone. For when You are the focus, true joy follows. In Jesus' name, amen.

Love in Action . . .

Pray Matthew 6:33 out loud: "Seek first his kingdom and his righteousness" (NIV). In whatever pain you are facing today, turn to Him for comfort and peace.

Marriage is about giving God the glory in good times and bad.

WEEK 27

LEARNING TO LEAD WHERE YOU ARE

The heart of the discerning acquires knowledge,
for the ears of the wise seek it out.

PROVERBS 18:15, NIV

Before I became a husband, God used a room full of high school seniors to teach me how to lead with humility. It was my first year of teaching, and overnight I went from being a young, enthusiastic college graduate to an instructor responsible for guiding a class of teenagers who were only a few years younger than me. Every day brought a different challenge. Some students were confident and outspoken, while others were quiet and unsure, and some were navigating battles at home that I didn't even know about until months later.

It didn't take long to realize that leadership wasn't about having authority. It was about listening. It was about noticing who needed encouragement, who needed structure, and who needed a safe place to land. In that classroom I learned how to mediate conflict, how to slow down instead of reacting, how to ask questions instead of assuming, and how to stay steady when emotions were high. Teaching wasn't just a job for me. It was God's training ground.

What I didn't see then was how much that season would prepare me for marriage. All of those skills I learned in the classroom (patience, communication, problem-solving, and compassion) became essential once I met Stefanie. Teaching shaped my character long before I knew who my wife would be. It taught me that leadership is not about control or being right. Leadership is service. Leadership is humility. Leadership is choosing to love people well in the small daily moments.

We often think we'll become who God wants us to be once life "really starts" or once we meet the right person. But God builds us long before that. He uses our everyday responsibilities, friendships, frustrations, and workplaces to form the kind of husband we'll be in marriage. Leadership that honors God doesn't begin on your wedding day. It begins today.

Dear God, *thank You for every season that shapes me. Teach me to lead with humility, patience, and wisdom right where I am. Make me attentive to the people around me, and help me reflect Your heart in the way I treat them. I pray for my future wife today. Strengthen her in her calling, and surround her with people who affirm her gifts. Prepare her heart as You prepare mine, shaping us both into individuals who lead with grace and honor. Grow us in maturity, teach us to listen, and help us follow Your voice in every decision. And when the time is right, bring us together in unity and purpose. In Jesus' name, amen.*

Love in Action . . .

Practice leadership today by listening first. Ask someone intentional questions and look for a way to serve them.

Lead where you are today.

WEEK

28

STRENGTH WRAPPED IN GENTLENESS

A servant of the Lord must not quarrel
but must be kind to everyone, be able to teach,
and be patient with difficult people.

2 TIMOTHY 2:24

Gentleness may seem like weakness, but in reality, it is one of the most powerful attributes you can cultivate if you want a strong marriage. Gentleness has the ability to unlock your wife's heart, build trust, and create an atmosphere where love and unity thrive.

I never thought of myself as someone who needed to work on gentleness. But like most men, I can speak bluntly without realizing how my tone comes across. I might sound frustrated or firm when I don't mean to. In my single years, this was never really a problem. But once I got married, I quickly saw that my tone mattered. Something as simple as "Yes, I'll do the dishes" could come out sounding harsh, even when I wasn't upset. After seeing Stefanie's reaction, though, I knew I needed to soften my response. I didn't want my wife to misunderstand my feelings or be hurt by my tone.

So how do you grow in gentleness? You start small. Be kind with your words. As Ephesians 4:15 directs us, we should speak the truth in love. You don't have to withhold the truth, but you can share it in a caring way. Practice with your roommates, your family, or your friends. Pay attention to how your tone shapes the message.

Gentleness is not weakness. It's a form of strength. It will open your future wife's heart in ways nothing else can. And the truth is, it takes far more strength to respond with gentleness than to lash out with frustration. The gentler you are in your marriage, the stronger you prove yourself to be.

Dear heavenly Father, *thank You for showing us through Jesus that gentleness is true strength. I ask You to grow a spirit of gentleness in me. Teach me to be mindful of my words and tone so my words build others up rather than tear them down.*

I lift up my future wife to You. Help her to be gentle with herself—to speak life over her body, her gifts, and her future. When she is tempted to be critical or harsh, remind her to speak words of hope and peace.

Let gentleness be a cornerstone of our marriage one day. Shape both of us now so we can carry grace into the covenant we will share. Protect us from the lies of the enemy that stir impatience, anger, or harshness. Lead us into Your truth and make us unwavering in the way we love. In Jesus' name, amen.

Love in Action . . .

Before you respond to someone today—at work, at home, or with friends—pause and choose gentle words over harsh ones.

Real strength shows up in gentleness.

WEEK

29

BUILDING A GOD-FIRST HOME

As for me and my family, we will serve the LORD.

JOSHUA 24:15

One of my favorite verses is Romans 12:2: "Do not conform to the pattern of this world, but be transformed by the renewing of your mind" (NIV). What I love about this verse is the call to resist being influenced by the world and to instead let our minds be renewed by Christ.

When I think about building a home that truly serves the Lord, I want everything to rest on the foundation of Christ. For Stefanie and me, one of the ways we've chosen to do this is in how we spend our mornings. Every single day, before we do anything else, we open our Bibles and spend time in prayer. Even if we have an early start, we set our alarms so our time with God is never compromised.

It wasn't always like this. In my single years and even early in our marriage, I thought I had enough knowledge of God to lead our marriage well. But I quickly learned that without that daily time with Him, I was quicker to lash out, I was less patient, and I was easily thrown off. What transformed me wasn't more willpower; it was daily time with the Father in His Word and in prayer. Before the distracting noise of work, my phone, or the world could flood my mind, I learned to let His truth set the tone for my day.

That daily choice reshaped my heart and made our home a sanctuary. A place where God's presence is welcome and felt. If you want to build a God-first home, start where you are. Pick up your Bible today. Read a verse or two. Build the habit. Over time, you'll see how God speaks, transforms your heart, and fills your home with His peace.

Heavenly Father, *thank You for being the solid foundation I can build my life on. I pray that my future marriage would be rooted in You alone. Give me courage to stand on Your truth and rely on it in both joyful and difficult seasons.*

I pray for my future wife. Strengthen her in this season. Surround her with godly friends, community, and a church that points her closer to You. If there are places where she is leaning on her own strength, gently redirect her into Your peace.

May both of us learn to build habits today that keep us close to You. Teach us to create space for prayer, to delight in Your Word, and to make our future home a place where Your presence dwells. Let our marriage always be anchored in Your love and truth. In the name of Jesus, amen.

Love in Action . . .

Pray over your home right now. Ask God to make it a space of peace filled with His presence. A God-first home starts before marriage.

The home I build now will shape the marriage I build later.

Father, help me grow
into the kind of husband
who loves sacrificially,
as Christ loved the church.

WEEK
30

DATING WITH DISCERNMENT

Enthusiasm without knowledge is no good;
haste makes mistakes.

PROVERBS 19:2

Dating out of desperation will always lead you down the wrong road. I know, because I have been there. After a breakup during my senior year of college, I was hurting and hoping to find someone to fill that void. In my desperation, I started looking in all the wrong places: the bar, the club, places I knew deep down weren't going to hold the kind of woman I was praying for.

The truth is, desperate people do desperate things. And their desperation is obvious. It's like wearing a Halloween costume. The only people the costume attracts are those who are just as desperate, and the cycle only leads to more emptiness. That's exactly where I found myself.

My lowest point came one night in Pasadena, trying to impress a bartender. I kept taking tequila shots, trying to prove I could handle the liquor. I couldn't. I ended up throwing up all over the bar and being kicked out. Sitting in the alleyway outside the bar, with vomit, garbage, and dirty puddles all around me, I hit rock bottom. That was the moment God got my attention. I realized I was chasing love in all the wrong places, and it was leading me nowhere.

From that point forward, I turned back to Him. I started seeking healing for my heartbreak. I began speaking truth over my future. I went back to church, even though I had been angry at God and staying away for a season. And as I consistently showed up week after week, I found community, healing, and people who pointed me closer to Him.

It didn't happen overnight, but eventually, in that very church, I met Stefanie. Not after a month or two but after years of showing up and letting God reshape me. Dating with discernment means knowing who you are in Christ and trusting that God has a good plan for your life. You don't settle. You don't compromise your values. You wait with wisdom and courage. Because desperation will get you nowhere, but discernment will lead you to your future wife.

Dear God, *thank You for being the source of wisdom in a world full of confusion. I pray for discernment for me and my future wife as we navigate the challenges of dating. Help us to make choices that honor You and protect our hearts from compromise.*

Guard my future wife from anyone who would try to take advantage of her. Surround her with friends and mentors who will point her back to You. Remind her that her worth is not measured by who texts her back or how many dates she goes on, but by Your promises and her identity in Christ.

Teach me the same thing. Let our conversations be seasoned with grace and truth. Give us the courage to set strong boundaries that protect our peace. Prepare our hearts for the covenant of marriage, and let every step we take draw us closer to You. In Jesus' name, amen.

Love in Action . . .

Before you swipe or message anyone today, say a prayer inspired by James 1:5. “Lord, give me wisdom.” Invite God into every interaction. Your worth is not in who responds or who doesn’t. God is with you through it all.

Wisdom is the foundation for dating well.

WEEK

31

DATING WITH INTEGRITY

The integrity of the upright guides them, but the unfaithful are destroyed by their duplicity.

PROVERBS 11:3, NIV

Before I met Stefanie, I went through a phase in dating that had nothing to do with purpose or prayer and everything to do with insecurity. A group of my friends had signed up for online dating, and I didn't want to feel left behind. I created a profile not because I was ready for a relationship, but because I wanted to prove something. I wanted to show that I could get dates too.

My motives were off, and it showed. I ended up going on a date with someone I knew I wasn't genuinely interested in. She was kind and sincere, and she showed up with real intention. But I showed up with pride. When the check came, I realized I had about forty-five dollars in my bank account, and the bill was forty-four dollars. I felt sick, and not just because of the money. I had compromised my character just to keep up an image. I had played with someone's time and heart to prove a point that didn't even matter.

On the drive home, God gently confronted me. He reminded me that dating is not a game. People are not props in your insecurity. And a man of God doesn't need attention to feel valuable; he knows he's already chosen by his Father.

That moment humbled me in the best way. I promised God, and myself, that when I dated again, I would date with intention. I would show up with honesty, integrity, and kindness. No pretending. No games. No proving my worth through people. And when I finally did date with purpose, God led me to the love of my life. Integrity didn't just shape my dating; it prepared me to be a husband.

If you're in a season of dating or waiting, let God shape who you are becoming. You don't have to force anything, pretend to be someone you're not, or chase validation. Your identity is secure in Christ, and that confidence will shape how you love one day.

Dear heavenly Father, *thank You for shaping my character and teaching me what integrity looks like in relationships. Guard my heart from insecurity, comparison, and the pressure to prove myself. Make me a man who dates with intention, honesty, and honor. I pray for my future wife today. Protect her heart, surround her with people who speak truth and confidence into her, and prepare her for a relationship rooted in You. Help both of us grow into people who love with integrity, wisdom, and courage. Lead us toward each other in Your way and Your timing. In Jesus' name, amen.*

Love in Action . . .

Before going on any date or making any dating decision, ask yourself, *Am I doing this out of intention or insecurity?* Let integrity make the choice for you.

Don't date to prove your worth.

WEEK

32

TRADE SCROLLING FOR LIVING

Be careful how you live. Don't live like fools, but like those who are wise. Make the most of every opportunity in these evil days.

EPHESIANS 5:15-16

One of the biggest traps the enemy sets in our modern world is distraction. If he can keep us distracted, he knows we'll miss God's goodness happening right before us. Social media is one of the easiest places for distraction and comparison to rob our attention. We scroll through engagement announcements, baby posts, new car pictures, and dream vacation memories, and suddenly our joy is replaced with envy. Or maybe we get lost in posts about politics, religion, or other divisive subjects. Before we know it, hours are gone, and our peace is stolen.

Because Stefanie and I work in relationships and share encouragement online, social media is part of our calling. But early on, it was a real struggle. We'd post something we felt proud of, only to feel discouraged when someone else's post went viral instead of ours. That constant comparison robbed us of our joy and became a trap.

So we set boundaries. Together we made a decision that changed everything: no social media on the weekends. It seemed risky at first for our jobs, but for the sake of our peace, it was worth it. That one boundary gave us the freedom to truly rest, to be present with each other, and to enjoy time together without distraction. Our weekends quickly became our favorite part of the week.

And here's the truth: Life is too short to waste time staring at a screen. God didn't create you to scroll endlessly. He created you to live fully. If you want more peace, ask Him to show you the boundaries you need to set. Choose today: Will you keep scrolling through other people's lives, or will you step into the abundant life He has for you?

Dear heavenly Father, *thank You for the gift of today. Teach me to live fully present with You and the people You've placed around me. Guard my heart against the trap of endless scrolling and comparison. Lift my eyes to see the beauty of Your creation, the blessings in my life, and the opportunities to connect with others in meaningful ways.*

I pray for my future wife. Break off any hold that social media might have on her heart. Remind her that her worth is found only in You—not in likes, followers, or online validation. Surround her with godly community that lifts her up and helps her walk in purpose.

For both of us, I ask for wisdom to create healthy rhythms and boundaries. Give us courage to put down our phones, to look up, and to engage in the real lives You've called us to live. May our marriage one day be marked by presence, joy, and purpose that overflow into the lives of others. In the name of Jesus, amen.

Love in Action . . .

If you struggle with boundaries, practice setting a timer for fifteen minutes on social media today. Use the rest of your time to do something that actually builds you up: read, lift weights, pray, or connect with a friend.

Instead of scrolling, start living.

WEEK

33

FIGHT FOR PURITY DAILY

Run from anything that stimulates youthful lusts. Instead, pursue righteous living, faithfulness, love, and peace.

2 TIMOTHY 2:22

When I look back on my single years, I see how much I struggled with lust and pornography. I'm not only remorseful for those habits, but I also now see how often I set myself up for failure. I felt stuck—in sin, in shame—and was too afraid to tell anyone about it. That shame kept me trapped in the same destructive cycle for years.

There is a battle over your purity every single day. It shows up in what you watch, what you look at online, the conversations you have, and the people you spend time with. Looking back, I can see how much I fed my temptation. I watched shows with TV-MA ratings that were filled with nudity and graphic images. These shows triggered lust and joked about women in degrading ways. None of that pointed me back to Jesus; it only pulled me deeper into sin.

If you're serious about your purity, you have to get serious about your boundaries. I had to stop watching those shows. I had to stop talking dirty about women. I had to step away from friends who only liked me when I was making poor choices. Those decisions weren't easy, but they changed my life for the better.

Purity isn't something you lose forever; it's something you can fight for and regain. When I chose to honor God with my thoughts, words, and habits, I found freedom and peace I didn't think was possible. And one of the greatest gifts of choosing purity is this: It's not only for you, but also for your future wife.

So take inventory of your life today. What shows, habits, or relationships are keeping you stuck? Make the decision now to pursue righteousness. When you fight for purity daily, you're not just saying no to sin; you're saying yes to God's best.

Dear God, *thank You for calling me to walk in freedom and purity. Guard my eyes, mind, and heart from anything that would lead me into lust or sin. Expose any habits or lies I've believed that pull me away from You, and give me the courage to replace them with truth.*

Help me to set strong boundaries around what I watch, the content I engage with online, and who I spend time with. Bring godly people into my life who will hold me accountable and encourage me to walk in righteousness.

I pray for my future wife. Protect her from those who would use her or lead her astray. Surround her with friends who value purity and encourage her to walk in Your ways. Guard her heart, mind, and body, and remind her that she is loved and cherished by You.

Lord, help both of us to see purity not as a burden but as a gift we gain each day as we walk with You. Teach us to trust You more deeply in this season, and prepare us for the marriage You've called us to. In the mighty name of Jesus, amen.

Love in Action . . .

Tonight, before bed, pray Psalm 119:37: "Turn my eyes from worthless things." Purity isn't a one-time choice; it's a daily fight.

Purity is a battle worth fighting every day.

WEEK

34

PREPARING FOR MARRIAGE ON PURPOSE

Plans fail for lack of counsel,
but with many advisers they succeed.
PROVERBS 15:22, NIV

When Stefanie and I got engaged, we knew one thing for sure: We wanted our marriage to last. We loved each other deeply, but we knew that love alone wasn't going to build the kind of marriage we were praying for. We wanted a relationship strengthened by wisdom, shaped by community, and guided by God.

So we decided early on that we would invest in our relationship before we ever walked down the aisle. One of the first things we did was enroll in a four-week preengagement class at our church. Every week we sat in a room with couples in different stages of dating and engagement, learning about expectations, communication, conflict, spiritual unity, and what it actually takes to build a Christ-centered marriage. Those weeks gave us language we still use today.

We also reached out to trusted counselors and mentors. We wanted people in our lives who wouldn't just agree with us, but who would lovingly challenge us and tell us the truth. One of the greatest blessings during that season was receiving preengagement counseling from Stefanie's professors at Fuller Theological Seminary. These were marriage and family therapists who were respected around the world, and sitting with them felt like one of the biggest gifts God could have given us. Their wisdom helped us understand our patterns, our wounds, and the places we needed to grow in order to truly love each other well.

Stefanie also led us through some of her past coursework. We sat on the couch together answering questions and talking through triggers, values, spiritual rhythms, and expectations for marriage. Those conversations weren't always easy, but they were foundational. They strengthened our trust. They prepared our hearts. They helped us walk into marriage with confidence instead of confusion.

Whether you're dating, engaged, or simply hoping for marriage one day, you can start preparing now. Invest in your character. Seek community over isolation. Invite mentors and counselors into your life. Let God shape you long before you say, "I do." Marriage doesn't just happen; it's built.

Dear God, *thank You for the gift of growth. Shape me into a man who prepares well, listens well, and loves well. Teach me to seek wise counsel and value the voices You've placed in my life. I pray for my future wife today. Surround her with mentors, community, and women who speak truth, encouragement, and wisdom into her. Strengthen her confidence in You, and prepare her heart for a Christ-centered marriage. Lord, prepare both of us for each other. Grow us in maturity, unity, and purpose. Make our future marriage strong, healthy, and rooted in You. In Jesus' name, amen.*

Love in Action . . .

Identify one person or couple you admire in marriage. Ask them one question this week: "What prepared you most before you got married?" Let their wisdom guide your next step.

Strong marriages start with intentional preparation.

WEEK

35 BOUNDARIES MAKE YOU STRONGER

A person without self-control
is like a city with broken-down walls.
PROVERBS 25:28

If you've ever seen *The Lion King*, you'll remember the powerful moment when Mufasa takes Simba to the top of Pride Rock to teach him a lesson. He tells Simba that everything the light touches is their kingdom. The camera pans to a vast and beautiful land stretching for miles. But off in the distance is a dark, shadowy land. When Simba asks about that area, Mufasa tells Simba he must never go there.

Like most of us, Simba wants to go exactly where he shouldn't. And when he disobeys his father's orders, he nearly loses his life. The boundary Mufasa had set wasn't to rob Simba of fun but to protect him from danger.

God works the same way. In His Word, God gives us boundaries, not because He's holding out on us, but because He loves us too much to watch us walk into destruction. Boundaries are His way of keeping us safe so we can fully become who He created us to be.

In my own life, I've found that boundaries bring freedom, not restriction. They give me clarity, helping me stay on the path that draws me closer to God. But when I ignore those boundaries, I end up hurting myself or others.

So ask yourself, *What boundaries do I need to set today?* Whether you're setting boundaries on your time, your phone, your friendships, or your choices, invite God into the process, and let Him lead you into a life of peace, safety, and freedom.

Dear heavenly Father, *thank You for loving me enough to give me boundaries that protect and strengthen me. Show me any unhealthy patterns or areas in my life where I'm overextending myself. Expose the places where I've been ignoring Your limits, and give me the courage to make changes. I submit my work, health, family, friendships, and future to You. Protect me from the trap of people-pleasing, and fill me with a spirit of truth, love, and service. Help me set healthy boundaries that allow me to love others out of the overflow of Your strength, not from a place of burnout or fear.*

I pray for my future wife as well. Guard her heart and her time from those who would take advantage of her. Give her wisdom to say no when she needs to and courage to say yes when You are leading her. Free her from comparison or fear of missing out, and root her identity in You.

Lord, teach us both to embrace boundaries as a gift from You. Let them shape us into the kind of husband and wife who can love fully, live wisely, and walk closely with You. In the name of Jesus, amen.

Love in Action . . .

Choose to set one boundary this week that will help you draw closer to God. Pray over it daily, and at the end of the week, journal about any differences you saw in your mind, body, and spirit.

The boundaries I set today protect my future tomorrow.

Father, give us courage
to put down our phones, to look
up, and to engage in the real lives
You've called us to live.

WEEK

36 WISE COUNSEL MAKES STRONG MEN

Without wise leadership, a nation falls; there is safety in having many advisers.

PROVERBS 11:14

I am so thankful for the wise men in my life. It is invaluable to have friends and mentors who speak life over you and point you toward the truth.

Back in college, I was dating someone when one of my mentors, a good friend I trusted, pulled me aside. He told me something I didn't want to hear. He had seen the woman I was dating spending time with another guy, and he was concerned. He could have kept quiet to avoid hurting me, but instead, he chose to tell me the truth out of love so I could make the best decision for my life. Unfortunately, I didn't listen. I couldn't imagine my girlfriend betraying me. But sure enough, my worst fear came true when she confessed. Looking back, I wish I had listened more closely to his counsel.

That moment showed me how important it is to have godly mentors in your life. Since then, I've prioritized surrounding myself with men I can trust who will tell me the truth even when it's hard. Their wisdom has made me stronger and a better husband to my wife.

If you want to grow into the man God is calling you to be, don't try to do it alone. Find mentors. Cultivate those relationships. Do whatever it takes to keep wise voices speaking into your life. Godly husbands aren't built in isolation; they're built by choosing humility and listening to counsel.

Dear heavenly Father, *thank You for the gift of wise counsel. I ask You to surround me with godly men who will speak truth into my life. Give me the courage to seek them out, the humility to listen, and the discernment to apply their wisdom. Protect me from pride, and give me a teachable spirit.*

I pray the same for my future wife. Place amazing women around her who will encourage her, guide her, and point her back to You in every season. Give her humility to listen and strength to walk in wisdom.

Lord, help both of us to lean on wise voices so we can navigate this season well. Use counsel to shape us into the husband and wife You've called us to be. Prepare us for a marriage rooted in truth and grace. In Jesus' name, amen.

Love in Action . . .

Call or meet with an older godly man this week. Ask him questions about faith and relationships and listen with humility.

A wise man seeks counsel,
not just opinions.

WEEK

37

BUILDING A LEGACY THAT OUTLIVES YOU

Their children will be successful everywhere;
an entire generation of godly people will be blessed.

PSALM 112:2

My dad is one of the greatest men I know. He spends his life with a clear purpose: to tell as many people about Jesus as possible and to pour into the next generation. He devoted his entire career to the same Christian school in Pasadena, California, where he served for decades. Over the years, he held nearly every role—teacher, coach, athletic director, dean, admissions director, and eventually the head of school.

But what stood out most during his career was how he lived. Our home became a safe haven for his students and athletes. Many of them came by long after graduation just to say thank you for the way he had impacted their lives. Watching his example was inspiring.

I hope I can leave a similar legacy. Not necessarily in a school setting, but in the way I live with the next generation in mind. I want my life to have purpose and be devoted to loving others, serving faithfully, and putting God at the center.

I know that much of the man I am today is because of my dad's example in our home. He continues to push me to serve others, to keep going when it's hard, and to love Stefanie in the best ways I can. His life reminds me that leaving a legacy isn't about grand gestures; it's about daily obedience.

So how do you build a legacy that outlives you? You serve God with humility. You ask Him what He wants for your life. You put others' needs before your own and trust that He will make a way, even when you don't see it yet. That's how my dad lives, and that's the kind of life I want to model. Start now by asking yourself what you can do today that will ripple into tomorrow. Small acts of faithfulness now will build the legacy that you will leave later.

Dear God, *thank You for the life You've given me. Open my eyes to see how You are always working behind the scenes, and give me a heart that overflows with gratitude. Teach me how to live with purpose that honors You and points others toward Your love. And Lord, show me how to make choices today that will leave a lasting impact tomorrow.*

I pray that You would stir the heart of my future wife as well. Encourage her to pursue her God-given dreams, to walk faithfully with You, and to use her life to make an eternal difference. Together, help us to pursue wisdom, discernment, and purposeful living. Let our marriage and actions leave a legacy that blesses future generations. May those who come after us see Your hand in our lives and be drawn closer to You because of it. In Jesus' name, amen.

Love in Action . . .

Pray for the next generation—future children, nieces, nephews, or younger men you'll influence. Ask God to make your marriage a blessing that will lay the path for generations to come.

Godly men build legacies that outlive them.

WEEK

38

WATCH AND LEARN FROM STRONG MARRIAGES

You yourself must be an example to them by doing good works of every kind. Let everything you do reflect the integrity and seriousness of your teaching.

TITUS 2:7

I'm grateful I grew up in a Christian home where my parents loved each other and weren't afraid to show it. As a kid, I was given a constant picture by them of the kind of marriage I wanted one day. I learned from my dad how to treat women and from both of my parents how to work as a team. They stuck together through every season, and even when they had disagreements, they always found their way back to unity. Their example of love and partnership has been one of the greatest blessings in my life, and I carry much of what I saw in their marriage into mine with Stefanie.

I'm also grateful for the wisdom Stefanie and I have received from other couples. When we were dating and newly married, we made it a priority to go to premarital counseling, attend marriage retreats, and learn from people who were a few steps ahead of us. We surrounded ourselves with godly couples who had strong relationships, and their influence made a huge difference in our young marriage.

One of the best things you can do for your future marriage is to learn from couples who are living theirs out well. Whether that's your parents, a mentor couple at church, friends, or even godly voices you follow online, find them. Watch their example. Ask questions. Learn from both their strengths and their struggles.

Yes, you'll learn plenty once you're married. But preparing ahead of time equips you and plants a foundation from which you can stand. And once you are married, don't stop learning. Keep surrounding yourself with couples who build you up, who speak life over your marriage, and who remind you that with God at the center, it's possible to thrive. A growth-minded posture now will bless your future more than you can imagine.

Dear God, *thank You for the gift of marriage and for the examples of healthy, godly couples that You've placed in the world. Teach me in this season what a strong marriage looks like, and bring couples into my life who will encourage me, speak truth, and model love that honors You.*

I pray for my future wife. Surround her with examples of godly marriages that inspire her and equip her to grow into the woman and wife You've called her to be.

Reveal to both of us any habits, patterns, or mindsets that could harm our future marriage, and give us the humility to grow in those areas now. Help us to remain teachable, to seek out wisdom, and to walk with couples who will lift us up rather than tear us down.

Thank You for the blessing of this season of preparation. May the lessons we learn now help us build a marriage that reflects Your love. In the name of Jesus, amen.

Love in Action . . .

Spend time with a married couple you respect. Notice how the husband loves his wife, and write down one takeaway you can bring into your future marriage.

Great husbands learn from other great husbands.

WEEK

39

DON'T HIDE; GET ACCOUNTABILITY

Confess your sins to each other and pray for each other so that you may be healed.

JAMES 5:16

The enemy loves to isolate you in your singleness. If he can get you alone, he can fill your mind with lies that you may even start to believe. I know this because the season I felt most stuck in sin was also the season I felt most alone. The shame was overwhelming, and I had no idea how to pull myself out.

By God's grace, He placed me in the right community, and that's when my freedom began to take root. For the first time, I opened up about my struggles, and instead of judgment, I found encouragement, truth, and support. Today, I have brothers who call me to higher standards, friends who push me past excuses and challenge me to live as the man God has called me to be.

If you're struggling with sin, especially hidden sin, don't try to fight it by yourself. It's ten times harder that way. Find community. Maybe it's a small group at church or a group of Christian men you spend time with. Look for people you can trust, who care enough to hold you accountable. If no one comes to mind, seek out a mentor, a counselor, or a trusted friend who can be that safe place, and don't overlook practical tools like accountability software to help guard your mind and heart online.

If you feel stuck in your sin, don't keep hiding. Stop making excuses. Take action today to honor God, and begin living in the light. Your future marriage will be stronger, and you can honor your future wife now by the choices you make today.

Dear heavenly Father, *thank You for Your forgiveness and grace. Thank You that no sin is too big for the cross. I ask that You make me quick to recognize where I fall short and quick to repent, so nothing stands between us. Wash away my shame and fill me with the freedom of Your love. Surround me with people who are trustworthy, godly, and full of Your Spirit, people who will hold me accountable, encourage me, and speak truth into my life. Reveal any hidden sin and give me the courage to bring it into the light.*

I pray for my future wife. Place strong, faithful friends and mentors in her life who will encourage her, guide her, and help her walk in purity and freedom. Keep her from hidden sin and remind her that her identity is found in You alone.

Prepare both of us now with friends and mentors who will strengthen our future marriage. Help us to build lives rooted in accountability, honesty, and grace. In the name of Jesus, amen.

Love in Action . . .

Share one area of struggle with a trusted brother in Christ this week. Invite him to check in so you don't fight alone.

Accountability makes me stronger, not weaker.

WEEK

40

PUT YOURSELF IN THE RIGHT ROOMS

Oh, the joys of those who do not follow the advice of the wicked, or stand around with sinners, or join in with mockers.

PSALM 1:1

One of the best decisions I made in my single years was finding a great church community. Attending a Sunday night service at a church in Los Angeles was a game changer. After trying several churches in the area, I was happy to finally land somewhere that fit the season I was in.

This church had a thriving singles and young adult ministry. After service, everyone would gather across the street where there was live music, a coffee bar, and plenty of space to hang out. For the first time in a long time, I found myself looking forward to church, not just for the service but for the community and the chance to connect with new people.

What started as a weekly visit turned into months and then years of consistently showing up. Then one Sunday, I ran into someone I had never seen before. Stefanie. Meeting her that night changed everything. God used my choice to keep showing up to introduce me to the love of my life.

That experience taught me something simple but powerful. If you want to meet the woman God has for you, put yourself in the places where she might be. Be intentional. If you've already found a church community, dive deeper. If you haven't, step out of your comfort zone and try a few until you find a good fit. Surround yourself with people who are chasing after God, and watch how being part of that community changes your life. You never know—your future wife might be waiting there too.

—

Dear heavenly Father, *thank You for the gift of godly community. Thank You for placing people in my life who point me back to You and encourage me in my walk. Help me never to take those relationships for granted. Lead me to the right places, the right rooms, and the right communities where I can grow in faith, build strong friendships, and prepare for the future You have for me. Give me humility to listen, wisdom to discern, and courage to step outside of my comfort zone.*

I pray for my future wife as well. Surround her with a community that lifts her up, speaks life over her, and protects her from harm. Guide her into relationships that strengthen her faith and remind her of who she is in You.

Lord, help both of us release any past pain or hidden sin that holds us back, and lead us into communities where Your truth and love are spoken. May those places shape us, prepare us, and draw us closer to You and to each other. In Jesus' name, amen.

Love in Action . . .

Join one place where godly men and women gather: a church group, Bible study, or serving team. Be present where God's best can be found.

The rooms I choose shape the future I build.

WEEK

41

LEARN FROM MEN WHO'VE GONE BEFORE YOU

Walk with the wise and become wise; associate with fools and get in trouble.

PROVERBS 13:20

As a kid, I worked hard to get what I wanted, sometimes by making deals with my parents and other times by trying to pin them against each other. I'll never forget the time I wanted a video game. I asked my mom about it first, and she said no, pointing out the cost. So I went straight to my dad, hoping to win him over.

Instead of asking him directly for the game, I started complaining about my mom. I said something along the lines of "I can't believe she won't get me that game. She's so lame." My dad stopped me in my tracks. He looked me in the eye and said, "Don't you ever talk about your mother that way. She is my wife, and I love her more than anyone else in this family. If you disrespect her, you're also disrespecting me."

At first, I was shocked by what my dad said. But then it sank in. My dad's world didn't revolve around me; it revolved around the covenant he had made with my mom. That order was right, biblical, and good. And instead of making me feel less loved, it made me feel more secure.

From that day forward, I watched my dad model what it meant to prioritize his wife, to support her, uplift her, and cheer her on. Loving her first and us second. That example set something in order for me, shaping the kind of husband I wanted to be.

It also taught me to pay attention to the wisdom of men who have gone before me. There's so much to learn, not only from their successes but also from their failures. If you want to grow into the husband and man God has called you to be, don't try to figure it all out on your own. Learn from those who've already walked the path.

Dear God, *thank You for the men You've placed in my life. I ask that You continue to place me in front of wise, godly men who can speak truth into me. Give me humility to listen, courage to ask questions, and wisdom to apply what I learn. Break down any barriers in me that keep godly people at a distance, and teach me how to build lasting relationships with those who will sharpen me.*

I pray for my future wife. Place strong, faith-filled women in her life who can pour into her and share wisdom from their journeys. Help her to pursue those relationships, learn from them, and grow into the woman and wife You've called her to be.

Teach both of us to honor those who've gone before us by listening well, receiving wisdom, and putting it into practice. Use this season to shape us into the kind of husband and wife who build a marriage rooted in humility, wisdom, and love. In the name of Jesus, amen.

Love in Action . . .

Ask a married man you respect one question: "What's the best advice you'd give your single self?" Write his answer down and apply it.

Wisdom multiplies when I learn from others.

Father, may the lessons we learn now help us build a marriage that reflects Your love.

WEEK

42

YOU ARE NEVER ALONE

Don't be afraid, for I am with you. Don't be discouraged, for I am your God. I will strengthen you and help you. I will hold you up with my victorious right hand.

ISAIAH 41:10

I'll never forget the smell of that old leather chair. Dust floated through streaks of sunlight in a dark room, where I sat for what felt like endless hours. My life had fallen apart—a breakup, the loss of my dream, and the passing of my grandpa. With no energy to move forward, I left my job, missed classes, and sank into isolation.

The irony was, I lived in a crowded house with seven other guys, but I had never felt more alone. Day after day I sat there, wallowing in pain, telling myself my life was over. Nights weren't better. I would try to sleep while my roommate had his girlfriend over, and the loneliness only deepened. The lie I believed was that nobody cared and that even God had left me. Maybe you've been there too. Maybe you're there right now.

The turning point came when I finally decided to take one step. Just one. I told myself, "I'm going back to class." I didn't have the strength, but God did. Looking back, I see that I was never truly alone. In every tear, in every moment of despair, God was right beside me, holding me up when I couldn't stand on my own.

Loneliness in singleness or heartbreak can feel suffocating. But you are not alone. The God who promises to strengthen you is with you right now. You don't need to see the whole path, just the next step. Let Him in, and He'll lead you to exactly where He wants you to be.

Dear Lord, *thank You that You never leave me nor forsake me. Even in the loneliest moments, You are near, and I can lean on Your strength. When I feel isolated, remind me of Your presence and give me the courage to take one step at a time toward the life You've called me to live. Help me find community and choose action over excuses so that I can grow into the man You've designed me to be. Prepare me to love my wife from a place of wholeness and security in You.*

I also pray for my future wife. When she feels lonely, draw her close to Your heart. Remind her that she is never alone, that You are her comforter, protector, and friend. Surround her with people who will speak truth and hope over her life.

Help both of us break free from loneliness by finding true connection in You. Thank You that Your victorious hand holds us up and guides us. In the name of Jesus, amen.

Love in Action . . .

When loneliness hits today, pause and read Psalm 23 out loud. Let it remind you of the Shepherd who never leaves you. Take one small step toward trusting God with your future, allowing Him to guide you where He wants to take you.

You may feel lonely, but you are never alone in Christ.

WEEK

43 BROTHERS WHO SHARPEN YOU

Encourage each other and build each other up,
just as you are already doing.
1 THESSALONIANS 5:11

For many years, I struggled to find brothers who would build me up and sharpen me spiritually. Pursuing friendships has not always come easy for me, and past wounds have made me hesitant to let people come close. But over the last decade, I've prioritized pursuing those kinds of relationships, and God has blessed me with some wonderful brothers.

When Stefanie and I moved to Pittsburgh four years ago, we had to start over with community, which was difficult. After a couple of years, we found a Bible study group at our church, and it changed everything. One of the men in that group has been instrumental in my life. He has encouraged me, uplifted me, and called forth the best in me as a man of God.

I've often told that Bible study that I believe God brought me to Pittsburgh, at least in part, for that group. They've spoken life over me like never before. They've been there for Stefanie and me in some of our darkest times, lifting us up with understanding, care, and grace. In that group, I know I can show up as myself, and if I start speaking lies over my life, they won't let me stay there. They always point me back to God's truth.

It is powerful to have brothers like that. And it has been healing for me after years of struggling to find authentic friendships. If you don't have brothers who sharpen you, I encourage you to seek them out. Find men who will speak the truth in love, who will carry you when you're weak, and who will encourage you when you need it most. Don't neglect brotherhood. Cultivate it. You should not try to go through life alone.

Dear heavenly Father, *thank You for the blessing of true friendship. I'm grateful for the men in my life who encourage me, sharpen me, and point me back to You. I ask You to continue bringing brothers like this into my life, men who will stand on Your truth and walk with me through both the good and hard seasons. Give me discernment to recognize relationships that aren't healthy and the wisdom to set boundaries so that negative influences don't take root in my heart. Help me love people well while protecting who I am.*

I pray the same for my future wife. Surround her with women of faith who will speak life over her, encourage her, and remind her of her worth in Christ. Protect both of us from unhealthy friendships, and lead us into communities that strengthen our walks with You.

Lord, help us to cultivate relationships that sharpen us, heal us, and call forth the best of who You created us to be. May we always point one another, and our friends, back to Your truth. In the name of Jesus, amen.

Love in Action . . .

Text a brother in Christ and ask, "How can I pray for you this week?" Strength is built when men sharpen each other.

Iron sharpens iron—real men sharpen each other.

WEEK

44

BUILDING A HOME FOR TOMORROW

Let's not get tired of doing what is good. At just the right time we will reap a harvest of blessing if we don't give up.

GALATIANS 6:9

Like many people, I always dreamed of the fairy-tale version of marriage. I pictured the house with the white picket fence, kids running through the yard, and a beautiful wife to come home to. But what I didn't envision is what it might take to reach those dreams. Though I longed for marriage, the habits I had built in my single years were actually preparing me for more singleness, not a strong marriage.

Back then, I stayed up late every night, ate unhealthy food, played video games for hours, and ignored spending time with God. I wondered why my life wasn't heading toward the marriage and future I wanted.

I'll never forget a sudden realization after a long *World of Warcraft* raid. I had been up past 3 a.m., losing battle after battle, when it dawned on me that all the gear and stats on my character meant nothing in real life. I didn't want to be a knight in a video game. I wanted to be someone's knight in shining armor in real life.

That's when I started to get serious about my habits. I began taking better care of myself, getting to bed earlier, and seeking out a community that built me up. Slowly, things shifted. I found a better job. I discovered an amazing church. I made new friends. And God began to move in ways I couldn't have orchestrated on my own.

Here's the truth: If you want a healthy marriage, career, or family in the future, start building the right habits today. The small choices you make now are building the home you'll one day live in. When you submit your heart to God and take daily steps in the right direction, He can turn even the smallest habits into a harvest of blessing.

Dear heavenly Father, *thank You for loving me unconditionally and surrounding me with people who speak life into me. Today, I lift up my habits to You. Reveal the areas where I need to grow so I can become the husband and father You are calling me to be. Break down any strongholds the enemy has over my thoughts, body, or future, and give me strength to walk in freedom.*

Show me which habits to start building now, and give me the discipline to follow through. Place people in my life who will encourage me, challenge me, and hold me accountable to live in alignment with Your truth.

I pray the same for my future wife. Help her identify and release any unhealthy patterns, and give her the courage to practice healthy boundaries in her relationships. Strengthen her with peace as she submits every part of her life to You.

Lord, teach both of us to build the marriage and family we want tomorrow by choosing obedience and wisdom today. Shape our hearts to look more like Yours, and help us to persevere in doing good, trusting that in Your timing, we will reap a harvest of blessing. In the name of Jesus, amen.

Love in Action . . .

Choose one small habit to practice now, like praying over meals, budgeting weekly, or putting your phone away before bed. These habits will shape your home later and benefit your marriage.

The habits I train for today will build my home for tomorrow.

WEEK

45 FAITH OVER FEAR, EVERY TIME

Be strong and courageous! Do not be afraid and do not panic before them. For the LORD your God will personally go ahead of you. He will neither fail you nor abandon you.

DEUTERONOMY 31:6

God has done many amazing things in our marriage, and one of the greatest themes of our journey has been learning to choose faith over fear.

When Stefanie and I launched our business and ministry in 2016, I felt dreams come alive in me that I thought had died after my back injury. I discovered a new sense of purpose and vision for how God could use us to impact lives and transform relationships. By the end of 2019, after years of growth, I was able to quit my job as a teacher and athletic director. It felt like God had opened a door, and we stepped through it with excitement and expectation.

But what came next was one of the hardest seasons of our lives. In 2020, the world shut down. Practically overnight, every source of income we had was cut off. Fear rushed in as we faced uncertainty. It would have been easy to give up, to take matters into our own hands, and to walk away from what God had called us to.

Instead, we pressed deeper into obedience. We prayed. We listened. We trusted God to provide, even when it felt impossible. And He did. He made a way for us in the middle of lack and uncertainty. He reminded us that if He called us to it, He would see us through it.

We still face hard seasons today, but we've learned something invaluable: Fear doesn't get the final say. God does. And when you partner with Him, He gives you the strength to keep going, even when everything around you feels shaky. Choose faith over fear, every single time.

Dear heavenly Father, *thank You for the strength You give me each day to walk out Your purpose for my life. Keep teaching me to rely on Your strength and not just my own. Show me the areas where I am clinging to self-reliance, and help me surrender them fully to You.*

I pray against every spirit of fear that tries to hold me back. Replace it with courage, boldness, and deeper trust in You. Teach me to fear You alone, not the opinions of people. When fear creeps in, remind me to run to prayer, Your Word, and godly community for strength.

I lift up my future wife as well. Guard her heart from fear and fill her with courage to stand firm in Your truth. Strengthen her faith so she knows that You are with her and will never abandon her.

Together, help us to build lives of faith that show in our choices, our actions, and our obedience. Remind us in every season that You are in control and that we can trust You fully. In Jesus' name, amen.

Love in Action . . .

When fear about the future hits, quote 2 Timothy 1:7 out loud: "God has not given [me] a spirit of fear and timidity, but of power, love, and self-discipline." Speak faith until your fear backs down.

Fear doesn't lead me—faith does.

WEEK

46

GRATITUDE BUILDS STRENGTH

Be thankful in all circumstances, for this is God's will for you who belong to Christ Jesus.

1 THESSALONIANS 5:18

I've learned that gratitude doesn't usually appear in the big, dramatic moments. It grows in the quiet ones. Most mornings, when I sit with God and open my Bible, I feel this wave of thankfulness wash over me. I think about Stefanie, our home, my family, and the people God has placed in my life. Even the simple things hit me: a warm bed, a safe place to live, a cup of coffee, sunlight coming through the window.

Those small reminders have shaped me more than I ever expected. They've trained my heart to notice what's good instead of what's missing. Gratitude has become one of the ways God centers me and keeps me grounded, especially in seasons when life doesn't look the way I'd hoped.

Years ago, I began a simple practice: thanking Him for three things every single day. It didn't matter how small they seemed (at first my list included coffee, football, and cheeseburgers); it just mattered that the daily habit began reshaping my heart. And over time, the practice grew.

Now, I write in a gratitude journal every morning. I take note of what God has done, what He is doing, and what I'm hopeful for. It's completely changed how I view the day ahead of me. Instead of beginning from a place of lack, I begin with abundance.

Gratitude has made me stronger. It gives me joy, peace, and resilience against the enemy's lies. When fear or disappointment shows up, gratitude reminds me that God has already given me everything I need to face it. Gratitude doesn't just change how you see your circumstances; it changes how you live.

Dear heavenly Father, *thank You for the blessings You've placed in my life. Today I pause to thank You for three specific things: __________, __________, and __________. Open my eyes to see the countless ways You provide for me, protect me, and show me Your love every single day.*

Reveal any pride, bitterness, or ungratefulness that lingers in my heart, and replace it with thanksgiving and praise. Help me to choose gratitude when fear, comparison, or disappointment tries to steal my joy. Teach me to start each day with thankfulness so I can live from a place of abundance.

I lift up my future wife as well. Cultivate a grateful heart in her. Help her to thank You for her body, her mind, her family, her community, and every way You are at work in her life. Guard her from believing that You are holding out on her. Instead, remind her daily of Your goodness and faithfulness.

May gratitude be the foundation of our marriage, shaping our words, our attitudes, and the way we see one another. Thank You for every blessing, Lord. You are worthy of all my praise. In the name of Jesus, amen.

Love in Action . . .

Before bed tonight, thank God for three things about your single season. Gratitude trains your heart for joy.

Gratitude brings joy and shapes the way you live.

WEEK

47

MARRIAGE IS MINISTRY, NOT JUST ROMANCE

He called his twelve disciples together and began sending them out two by two, giving them authority to cast out evil spirits.

MARK 6:7

I love spending every moment with Stefanie. Cultivating romance in our relationship has been one of the greatest joys of my life. But I've also come to learn that marriage is just as much a ministry as it is a romance.

Doing things purposefully together has stretched me as a man and as a husband. One example came during the height of the pandemic in 2020, when we were living in Los Angeles. Our church called and asked if we would help hand out meals to families in need. At first, I was hesitant. Everything regarding COVID-19 was uncertain, and I didn't want to put us at risk. But Stefanie didn't hesitate for a second. She saw it as an opportunity to do God's work.

So we went. Our church at the time was Angelus Temple, the home of the Dream Center, which feeds thousands of people across Los Angeles every month. When we pulled into the parking lot, I knew it was exactly where we were supposed to be. Stefanie practically jumped out of the car, running to the line to hand out food, pray with people, and encourage families. Watching her serve so wholeheartedly lit something in me.

That day wasn't glamorous. It was messy, chaotic, and a little scary. But it was also beautiful. It reminded me that sometimes the greatest romance in marriage is serving God together, pouring out love for Him by pouring into others.

When you learn to serve as a team, your marriage grows stronger than ever before. Don't wait until marriage to start living this way. Begin cultivating a servant's heart now. Look for ways to bless others, and bring that posture of ministry into your future marriage.

Dear God, *thank You for giving me a purpose and calling me to be part of Your work on earth. Help me to take that purpose seriously, walking in obedience each day to love and serve others well. Reveal people in need, Father, and give me wisdom in how to bless them.*

I pray the same for my future wife. Give her a servant's heart, Lord, and show her the unique people You're calling her to love. Strengthen her gifts, and give her courage to use them boldly for Your glory.

When we come together in marriage, help us see our love not only as a romance but also as a ministry. Teach us to minister to each other and to stand united in ministering to others. Make our marriage a testimony of Your love, and let it overflow into service that impacts lives for eternity. In the name of Jesus, amen.

Love in Action . . .

Think of one way you'd like to serve God as a husband. Start practicing it now, whether that may be leading prayer, giving generously, or serving in church.

**Marriage is more than love.
It's a mission together.**

Father, help both of us break free from loneliness by finding true connection in You.

WEEK

48

ABUNDANCE IN CHRIST, NOT SCARCITY IN FEAR

This same God who takes care of me will supply all your needs from his glorious riches, which have been given to us in Christ Jesus.

PHILIPPIANS 4:19

During my single years, especially right after my college breakup, I slipped into a scarcity mindset. In my pain, I clung tightly to what I had left and found it hard to trust God with my future.

It felt like the parable of the talents. Instead of multiplying what God had given me, I buried my dreams, convinced it was safer not to risk anything else. I stopped dreaming. I stopped believing. I settled into survival mode, existing from a place of fear rather than faith.

But this mindset kept me stuck. What eventually set me free was learning to unearth those buried dreams and lay them at God's feet. I asked Him to show me how to multiply the gifts He had given me, and when I did, everything started to change.

I got a new job. I found an amazing community. I began believing God's truth instead of the lies that I wasn't enough or that nothing good would work out for me. God opened new doors, revealed new opportunities, and breathed new life into me.

That's what happens when we stop living from a scarcity mindset and start receiving the abundance that is already ours in Christ. The shift begins with gratitude. Gratitude for what God has already done. Gratitude for what He is doing right now. Gratitude for the promises still to come.

You don't have to bury your dreams. Lay them at the feet of Jesus and trust Him to bring life, multiplication, and blessing to them in His timing. Abundance is already yours in Christ.

Dear heavenly Father, *thank You for being my provider and for supplying everything I will ever need in Christ Jesus. Help me focus my eyes on the blessings already in my life rather than on what I lack. Protect me from slipping into a scarcity mindset, and remind me that in You I always have more than enough. Show me any places where I've been relying more on the world's provisions than on Yours, and reset my priorities so they line up with Your truth.*

I pray for my future wife. Teach her to depend fully on You for provision while also walking in wisdom and diligence with the responsibilities You've given her. When times get hard or resources feel slim, help both of us to rely on You. Strengthen me to lead our marriage with faith, not panic, and to continually point my wife back to You as our ultimate provider.

You are more than enough for us, Lord. We claim Your promise that You will supply all of our needs according to Your glorious riches. Help us to trust You with every area of our lives and to live each day in the abundance of Christ. In Jesus' name, amen.

Love in Action . . .

What do you lack right now? What dreams have you buried? Surrender these desires to God and pray for His promises for your life.

Scarcity is a lie. God provides more than enough.

WEEK

49

TAKING THOUGHTS CAPTIVE

We take captive every thought to make it obedient to Christ.

2 CORINTHIANS 10:5, NIV

I've loved football my whole life, and back in our first year of marriage, the Cowboys were in the playoffs. It was a high-stress game, the kind where every play feels like it's carrying the weight of the season. At the end of the game, the refs overturned what I believed was the game-winning catch, and something snapped inside me. I yelled, paced, and let frustration take over.

When I finally looked over at Stefanie, she wasn't angry. She was quiet. Uncomfortable. Taken aback by how intense my reaction had been. Not because she thought I was a bad person, but because the moment revealed something deeper in me that neither of us expected.

Later, as I cooled down, I realized what had actually happened. My reaction wasn't really about football. It was about the toxic thoughts I'd carried for years, thoughts from my past injuries, lost dreams, and moments I felt like a failure. Somewhere along the way, I let myself believe that winning meant I was worth something, and losing meant I wasn't. That lie had been hiding under the surface, and the game simply exposed it.

But here's the grace of God: He used that moment to reveal a place in my heart He wanted to heal. As I sat with Him, I realized I didn't have to live at the mercy of old thoughts, emotions, or false identities. In Christ, I'm not defined by wins or losses, success or failure. I'm defined by who He says I am. Learning to take thoughts captive has changed everything, not just in my own life, but in how I lead, love, and protect my marriage. A man who knows the truth about who he is in Christ becomes a man who can speak life, stability, and truth over his spouse.

—

Father, *thank You for showing me the places in my heart where lies try to take root. Teach me to recognize toxic thoughts quickly and to bring them under the authority of Your truth. Help me to see myself the way You see me and to walk in a confidence that comes from You alone. I pray for my future wife too. Guard her mind with Your peace and protect her from lies that try to steal her joy or identity. Prepare both of us to build a marriage founded on truth, a relationship where we speak life over each other and point one another back to You. In Jesus' name, amen.*

Love in Action . . .

Pay attention to one moment today when your thoughts drift toward fear, insecurity, or frustration. Stop and pray, "Jesus, help me take this thought captive. Show me Your truth instead."

My thoughts don't lead my life. God's truth does.

WEEK

50 PRAY FOR A MARRIAGE THAT LASTS

Didn't the LORD make you one with your wife? In body and spirit you are his. And what does he want? Godly children from your union. So guard your heart; remain loyal to the wife of your youth.

MALACHI 2:15

From the very beginning, Stefanie and I have made it a priority to invest in our marriage. We've always seen it as something worth pouring into—a gift we waited for and one we never want to take for granted. Over the years, we've gone to marriage retreats, conferences, and counseling sessions, and we've learned from mentors who have walked the road before us.

One retreat that left a lasting impression on me was at Hume Lake in the Sierra Nevada mountains of California. It's a breathtaking place, set against the backdrop of the beautiful lake. Each year, Christian marriage leaders came to speak, and we always left encouraged and challenged to grow deeper together.

One of the most moving parts of the retreat was an exercise where all the couples in the room raised their hands. The leader would say, "If you've been married for more than one year, keep your hand up." Then five years. Then ten. Then twenty. It went all the way up to sixty and even seventy years. Every time, there were couples in the room who had been married for decades, living nearly their whole lives together.

I was always blown away by that. Imagine sharing that much life with one person, through highs and lows, victories and trials. And yet, when asked how they made it last, the couples always came back to the same answer: They kept investing in their marriage. Even after sixty years, they were still showing up at retreats, still wanting to learn how to love each other better. That kind of humility is what makes a marriage last—the willingness to grow, to forgive, to learn, and to keep showing up.

That's the kind of marriage I want. And that's the kind of marriage you can build if you start now. Don't wait until you're married to prepare. Grow in humility, kindness, and grace today. Learn from those who have gone before you, and keep learning after you're married. A marriage that lasts is not built in a moment. It's built day after day with love, humility, and a heart submitted to God.

Dear heavenly Father, *thank You for the season I am in right now. Help me to be fully present in it, trusting that You are using today to prepare me for tomorrow. I pray for a marriage that lasts, a marriage built on Your Word, Your love, and Your strength. Teach me humility, kindness, and perseverance so that I can be the kind of husband who invests daily in the relationship You give me.*

I pray for my future wife as well. Strengthen her faith and give her a heart that seeks You first. Teach her to bring every part of our marriage to You so that together we can remain loyal, united, and strong. When challenges come, help us rely on You. When discouragement creeps in, encourage our hearts. Surround us with godly community that will support us, pray for us, and hold us accountable. Help us never to stop learning and growing together. Help us want a marriage that endures for a lifetime and brings You glory in every season. In the name of Jesus, amen.

Love in Action . . .

Pray this out loud: "Lord, prepare me to be faithful to one woman for a lifetime. Make me a man who will invest in my marriage and daily submit to You."

God's design for marriage is to last a lifetime.

WEEK 51

PURITY: WOMEN ARE NOT OBJECTS

God's will is for you to be holy, so stay away from all sexual sin. Then each of you will control his own body and live in holiness and honor—not in lustful passion like the pagans who do not know God and his ways.

1 THESSALONIANS 4:3-5

One of the first things I walk my clients through is whether they are struggling with pornography or filling their minds with images they shouldn't. It devastates your future when you consume things you were never meant to see. With a phone in your pocket, temptation is everywhere, and there will always be excuses if you allow yourself to believe them.

For years, I had no boundaries around what I watched, and pornography had a strong hold on me. I want to be clear: Women are not objects. They are not images to consume or bodies to use. They are people, made in the image of God, with dignity and purpose.

When God began breaking me free from that addiction, He also began renewing my mind. I started to remind myself that every woman has a story. She is someone's daughter. She is someone's future wife. She is someone's future mother. She is an image bearer of the Most High God. When you look through that lens, you see the depth of the depravity in objectifying them.

If this is your struggle, I want you to know two things. First, there is grace. Jesus died so you are not bound to this sin, and you don't have to let shame keep you trapped. Second, you can choose today to start seeing women as God intended—not as objects, but as daughters of the King of kings.

A real man walks in courage, strength, and self-control. Treat every woman the way you would want someone to treat your daughter one day.

Dear heavenly Father, *thank You for creating women in Your image, each one with dignity, purpose, and value. Thank You for the women in my life who inspire me, encourage me, and point me closer to You.*

Establish in me a pure heart and healthy vision. Guard my eyes and mind from anything that would lead me into lust or impurity. Expose any habits that keep me stuck, and give me the courage to set boundaries that protect me. Help me run from temptation and fill my mind with truth that renews me daily.

I pray the same over my future wife. Help her not to seek validation in the opinions of men but to find her worth and confidence in You alone. Teach her to honor You with her body, her words, and her life.

Prepare us both to honor each other in marriage. Help me to one day tell her, with full integrity, that she was worth the wait. Keep us pure in this season so that our future marriage can shine with holiness, honor, and love. In Jesus' name, amen.

Love in Action . . .

Today, unfollow any account that stirs up lust or treats women as objects. Set up a filter or blocker on your devices to protect your eyes and your heart. Train yourself to see women as God's daughters, not images.

God calls us to honor women, not dehumanize them.

WEEK

52

DREAM BIGGER WITH GOD

Now all glory to God, who is able, through his mighty power at work within us, to accomplish infinitely more than we might ask or think.

EPHESIANS 3:20

I never thought I'd write a book. In fact, once upon a time, I barely thought I'd finish reading one. That may sound crazy coming from someone who is now working on his sixth published book, but it's true. Growing up, I wasn't a strong reader. The only time I read was when my mom made a deal with me: For every hour I wanted to play video games, I had to read for an hour first. Smart move on her part.

I made it through high school reading as little as possible. The same goes for college. But grad school forced a reality check. I couldn't skate by anymore; I either had to read or drop out. It wasn't that I disliked what I was reading. It was the sitting still that I struggled with. But eventually, I pushed through and began reading regularly. Now, not only have I read many books, but I've written several myself.

It's funny to write about the dreams God puts on our hearts. My dream growing up was to be a professional athlete, traveling Europe and playing internationally. But God's dream for my life was much bigger. Little did I know that He would give me the opportunity to reach millions of people online with encouragement about relationships.

Here's what I've learned: Don't get so locked in to how you think your life should look that you miss God's bigger picture. When I injured my back my senior year of college and watched my dream of professional basketball crumble, it was devastating. But God had His plan. God can do more with a little obedience than we can with years of striving. This very book you're reading is evidence of what He can do with a surrendered dream.

If you're holding on to a vision for your life, let God shape it. He may take you somewhere you never imagined, and it will be infinitely better than what you had planned. And as He forms you into the man you're becoming, He may be preparing a woman who will walk beside you in purpose, prayer, and unity. God wastes nothing. Even this season is part of the love story He's writing.

Dear heavenly Father, *thank You for the dreams You've placed on my heart. Teach me to dream bigger with You. Help me take faithful steps each day toward what You're calling me to, walking in obedience and trust. Give me courage to stop making excuses and to take action.*

I pray for my future wife. Encourage her to pursue the dreams You've given her, fill her with peace, and give her grace to accomplish everything You've called her to do.

Show both of us how to grow in this current season and how to prepare for the future You're writing for our lives. Teach us now to dream big with You over our future marriage, placing every plan in Your hands and trusting You to lead us. In the mighty name of Jesus, amen.

Love in Action . . .

Take ten minutes today to pray about your future marriage. Ask God to show you His vision. Write down anything He places on your heart, and begin taking action toward what He's calling you to.

God's dream for me is bigger than my own.

Acknowledgments

To my Lord and Savior Jesus Christ. You have never given up on me. You saw me while I was in my darkest pit and came in after me. Thank You for dying for me and giving me new hope in You. I owe my all to You. I love You.

To the woman of my dreams, Stefanie. You light up my life. Your passion for restored hearts is contagious. I would not have written this book if it weren't for you and your obedience to the call of God. Years ago, you brought hope to my life and helped restore my relationship with Jesus, and now it is the greatest honor of my life to be your husband. I am forever grateful for the dreams we share and working with you to help others. Thank you for being my best friend and the love of my life.

To my children, Shiloh and Asher, in heaven. Stefanie and I long to hold you in our arms, but we know you are with God. We love you and hope to honor you in how we love and serve others. We can't wait to see you in heaven. To any future children God might bless us with: You will be our redemption story. We love you already.

To my parents, John and Kay. Your love for each other, the romance, and the fun you continually cultivate show that love can last forever. Thank you for your support and encouragement in making this dream of ours come true. Stefanie and I feel every prayer, and we are so thankful for the ways you are there for us in both the good and difficult times. You motivate us to see the best in each other and to fight for each other in every circumstance.

To my in-laws, Ed and Susan Stack. I'm forever grateful for the love, sacrifice, example, and generosity you have shown since coming into my life. I am so thankful God chose you to be my in-laws. You have taught me so much about the servant heart of Jesus in your actions. Your work ethic and the way you pour your heart and soul into loving others is such an inspiration. I love you both so much.

To my brothers, Matt and Jesse. Thanks for being great brothers to Stefanie and me! You guys are such a gift. And to Alicia, my sister-in-law, and our niece and nephew, Shirah and Josiah: I am so thankful for each of you and appreciate the love and encouragement you always show me. Shirah and Josiah, I'm praying for your future husband and future wife. God has such amazing plans for you!

To my grandma Marcia. Thank you for your constant and consistent love and words of encouragement. You have always been a beacon of light and love. All my memories growing up with you make me smile. You are an inspiration for endurance and grace. You have shown me how to overcome and trust God no matter what season I am in. I am so honored to be your grandson.

To my grandpa Jim and grandma Anna (both in heaven). I love you so much and can't wait to see you in heaven. Thank you for always believing in me and for all the fun times we shared in Missouri.

To Stefanie's grandma Maryann "Nanny" Miller and grandpa Bob "Pappy" Miller (now in heaven), and to our Aunt Cindy. You are the most generous, loving humans. You continually think of others before yourselves. No matter what you have, you look for ways it can bless others. Pappy wrote Stefanie a letter a week for almost ten years, and we received many at the beginning of our marriage. I know his funny, caring way inspired Stefanie to write and go after our dreams. Nanny and Cindy, you continually support and love us and make this world a better place.

To Stefanie's grandpa Bill Stack and to her grandma Tris Stack and her Aunt Dee (all now in heaven). You continually spoke love and inspiration over us. You cultivated so much fun, joy, and unconditional love.

To Stefanie's sister, Cristina. I'm so grateful for you. To Daniel, my brother-in-law, and our nephews, Daxton and Kadan: We love you so much. You bring so much joy, laughter, and fun into our lives. I'm so proud of you, Daxton and Kadan. God has such amazing plans for your life! We are praying already for your future wives!

To my friends, family, and mentors. You are so valued and appreciated. I couldn't have done this project without you. We see you, and we love you so much. Thank you for believing in us. To Chelsea, Nick, Hudson, and Samuel. We love you guys beyond measure. Thanks for being such a faithful friend, Chelsea.

Christy Junod, thank you for loving Stefanie so well and fighting for us in prayer and encouragement. Your friendship means the world to us, and I love Logan, Everett, and Vivienne so much!

And to our Bible Study Fam: Brenna, Eileen, Tabitha, David, Justine, Jordan, Molly, Tyler, Dan, Dosalyn, Kelly, and Charles. Your encouragement and prayers have meant more to us than you could know.

To my extended family, the Stacks, the Kohls, the Carys, the Horns, the Finnys, the Rouses (and everyone else). We love you and thank God for each of you.

To my high school best friends, JJ, Dave, and Mike. Your friendship and support over the years mean the world to me. I love you all so much.

To my other brothers in Christ I love beyond words: Brandon, Andrew, Collin, Matt, Montell, Elijah, and to all our dear friends. You have each influenced my life in such powerful ways. I'm beyond grateful for each of you.

To pastors Dave D'Angelo, John Nuzzo, Matt Barnett, and Kurt Bjorklund. We thank God for you being our pastors throughout our walk with God! To our beloved sponsor children, Juan, Samantha, and Victor. We love you and believe in you!

To Sarah Atkinson and the team at Tyndale House Publishers. Thank you for believing in us, for investing in our dreams, and for helping us share our story with the world. Thank you for your intentional feedback, your kindness, and for crying with us, laughing with us, and pushing us to make this book the best it can be.

To Alex Field and The Bindery Agency. Working with you has allowed us to dream bigger and make a lifelong dream become a reality. We appreciate you for believing in us and for being our advocates throughout this process.

To our Cultivate Relationship, *Wholehearted Love*, and Waiting Well women and men, and to all those we have the huge honor of mentoring. We love you, Laura, Mirta, Michelle, Deanna, Sarah, Kristi, Alisa, Brenda, Makayla, Elisabeth, Senam, Katarina, Rachel, Hannah, Vienna, Chad, Victor, Tobius, Matthew. And to all the rest, we cherish you. Your courage, love, kindness, and growth are so inspiring. We love you and believe in you. We are so proud of you, and we know God is in the midst of redeeming everything in your life.

To our online community. You are loved beyond measure! God has an amazing plan for your life, and we hope this book inspires you to realize that you are not forgotten. The pain and heartbreak you have experienced are not the end of the story. God has so much in store for you! Thank you for your encouragement and support!

About the Author

Caleb Rouse and his wife, Stefanie, are best friends, partners in life and ministry, and passionate mentors who love walking with singles and couples toward God's best for their relationships. Having experienced both heartbreak and healing in their own journeys, they know firsthand the power of God's redemption in love stories. Their heart is to see others discover the same freedom, hope, and joy that they have found in Christ.

With their master's degrees in education (Caleb) and marriage and family therapy with an emphasis in theology (Stefanie), they combine biblical wisdom, counseling tools, and their own real-life story to encourage people in every stage of their relationships. Together, they lead online communities such as the Waiting Well Singles Community and Cultivate Relationship, where thousands find encouragement, prayer, and practical tools for love that lasts.

As authors of *Wholehearted Love* and the *52 Prayers for My Husband/Wife* series, and as the creators behind @calebjasonrouse, @stefanie.rouse, @ChristianSoulmates, and the *Wholehearted Love Podcast*, they share daily encouragement with hundreds of thousands around the world. Their vision is simple: to help people love out of the overflow of God's love, creating marriages and families that reflect His goodness.